# The Crocodile Man

# The Crocodile Man

*A Case of Brain Chemistry
and Criminal Violence*

André Mayer & Michael Wheeler

Houghton Mifflin Company Boston 1982

*Library of Congress Cataloging in Publication Data*

Mayer, André, date
  The crocodile man.

  Includes index.
    1. Insanity — Jurisprudence — Massachusetts. 2. Insane,
Criminal and dangerous — Massachusetts. 3. Chemistry,
Forensic. 4. Brain Chemistry. I. Wheeler, Michael,
date. II. Title.

| | | |
|---|---|---|
| KFM2966.6.M258 | 345.744'04 | 82–999 |
| ISBN 0–395–31840–8 | 347.44054 | AACR2 |

Printed in the United States of America

P 10 9 8 7 6 5 4 3 2 1

*For Pete, Kate, and Eve*

The crocodile serves man in many ways . . . Most especially he is a type and sign for us of our own unredeemed nature.

— EVELYN WAUGH

# Acknowledgments

WRITERS OFTEN MUST cast about for topics, shape them into proposals, and search for a willing publisher before they can embark upon a book. Thanks to the efforts of others, we fortunately were spared this burden. Steve Heims not only presented us with the idea for this project, through our mutual friend Jonathan Bayliss, but introduced us to a publisher ready to sponsor it. We hope the finished book confirms Steve and Jonathan's confidence in us.

The writing of the book was made much easier by the cooperation of those who were deeply involved in the criminal-insanity trial it describes. David Roseman, of Chaplin, Casner and Edwards in Boston, and Frank O'Boy, now in private practice in Taunton, Massachusetts, represented the defense and the prosecution, respectively. Both were extremely generous with their time and their insights. David was candid in discussing his role in the case, but he was scrupulous about not revealing confidential conversations he had with his client. He also introduced us to the defendant's father, Nicholas Decker, an endocrinologist who had an active role in designing the unusual biochemical defense, and to Mark Altschule, the specialist who treated the defendant and who testified at his trial. All of these people read earlier drafts of the book and corrected a number of mistakes. As each saw the case from a somewhat different perspective, they did have some contrasting opinions and interpretations. Any errors of fact or emphasis that remain, of course, are solely our responsibility.

We are similarly in debt to several people who helped see the project to its conclusion. Terry Hill and Candace Wheeler read initial drafts, and many of their suggestions are incorporated in this final revision. We are especially grateful to our editor, Dick McAdoo, who gently proposed changes that certainly have strengthened the book. Our thanks also go to Marty Geolfos, business manager at the University of Colorado School of Law, who supervised production of the manuscript on very short notice. Bill Pizzi, Associate Dean at Colorado, kindly arranged research help. Particular credit is due Kate Knickrehm, who was both energetic and resourceful in uncovering important material that somehow had eluded us.

ANDRÉ MAYER
MICHAEL WHEELER

*Boston, Massachusetts*

# Contents

# Preface

HOW IS IT THAT seemingly ordinary people can commit monstrous crimes? The notorious Son of Sam, whose random killings terrorized New York City, turned out to be an anonymous mail clerk. John Wayne Gacy looked like a model citizen to his suburban Chicago neighbors, yet in his basement were the corpses of more than two dozen young men he had methodically murdered. Mark Chapman, who shot ex-Beatle John Lennon, was described by Murray Kempton as looking "as blank as a milk bottle." Kempton calls Chapman "a reminder of the penalties we pay from our habitual neglect of apparently negligible people."

Violent crime is repelling yet somehow engrossing, particularly when it appears senseless and out of character. At one time society looked to demonology to explain such wickedness (an approach not wholly out of fashion today). More recently, Freudian theory taught that aberrational behavior may betray deep-seated emotional disturbances. Today, neurologists and pharmacologists are discovering physical triggers that, if tripped, can cause people to lose self-control.

On one level, the quest to understand crazy behavior has been no less than an inquiry into the ancient question of free will versus determinism. Who shall be responsible for his actions, and who shall be held blameless? But when madness results in crime, the issue is not only philosophical but pragmatic. While the medical profession continues to investigate causes of irrational behavior, judges and juries must make the ultimate diagnosis in specific cases.

When a defendant is charged with murder, acceptance or rejection of the insanity defense may be literally a matter of life and death. Even when it is clear beyond a reasonable doubt that the accused was insane at the time of the crime, a court may still have to decide whether the defendant has since recovered, and thus can safely be released. In many cases, of course, there is debate over the defendant's true mental state. A parade of experts, summoned by the prosecution and the defense, will challenge each other's methods and conclusions. When there is uncertainty, should the defendant be shielded by the traditional requirement that crimes be proven beyond reasonable doubt? On a broader level, how can we expect our courts to reach just verdicts in insanity cases when there is so much controversy in medicine over the nature of mental illness?

When the Commonwealth of Massachusetts prosecuted Charles Decker several years ago, the trial escaped public attention. Nonetheless, we believe that case signals a development in insanity cases that will be felt for years to come. Out of the blue, the defendant had brutally attacked two teen-age hitchhikers with a stonemason's hammer. Decker claimed insanity, but instead of relying on conventional psychiatric evidence to support his plea, his lawyer used the testimony of a specialist in the emerging field of brain chemistry and behavior. The defendant, it was claimed, suffered from a lesion in the limbic system, a primitive portion of the brain that exists in both man and the crocodile. It was a chemical dysfunction, the defense claimed, that caused Decker to lash out so viciously. The prosecution called its own expert, who testified that the defense's case was built on conjecture, not proven science. Everyone involved agreed that the only way to prove the lesion's existence conclusively would be through an autopsy on the defendant—and he was still very much alive.

The ambiguity of the Decker case was what sparked our interest. Was Decker's physician's diagnosis legitimate, or did the defendant merely act out of malice? Even if he did have some sort of brain damage, did that argue for releasing him or keeping him locked up? Could a trial judge, experienced in criminal law but unschooled in biochemistry, reasonably be expected to resolve issues on which prominent scientists cannot agree?

What began as a straightforward account of one criminal trial necessarily became a broader examination of the insanity defense, for the legal and medical problems raised in the Decker case have roots that go back for centuries. As the book evolved, we also became increasingly concerned with process as well as principle. Lawyers and physicians who confront insanity employ different methods and values. Truth in the laboratory and truth in the courtroom can be two quite different commodities. While we necessarily have been selective, we have attempted to relate the Decker case to other important insanity trials, past and present. Throughout the book we shuttle back and forth from the specific case to more general analysis. We hope that readers will be intrigued by these digressions rather than distracted by them.

The Decker case, of course, remains an organizing element of this book, and to the extent possible, we have tried to present the case largely as it unfolded before the court that decided it. Thus after a short introductory chapter, we turn in chapter 2 to the trial, specifically the prosecution's case against Decker. Chapter 3 describes the formulation of Decker's defense, and includes a brief history of the laws on which it rested. Chapter 4 is a parallel account of the medical investigation of Decker's condition, and the evolving scientific theories on which it was based. Law and medicine come together in chapter 5, which describes the courtroom presentation of the defense's case. The final chapter is an epilogue of sorts, describing not only the outcome of *Commonwealth v. Decker,* and the defendant's later experiences, but also presenting a look at the case's broader implications.

Through the generous cooperation of the participants in the trial—noted at greater length in the acknowledgments—we have had access to material that was not part of the public record. Out of consideration for the victims and the defendant—and their respective families—we have changed their names. We also altered the docket numbers of the indictment. Quotations used in describing the trial come directly from the official court transcript.

# The Crocodile Man

# 1. Crime

THE MORE VICIOUS the crime, the louder the cry for retribution. All violence is frightening, but gratuitous acts of brutality—crimes with no apparent motive, or where the victim is a stranger, or in which the acts are perverse—seem almost beyond comprehension. Judges and juries who mete out punishment have long considered not only the result of the crime but the manner in which it was committed. A Massachusetts statute provides that a person convicted of murdering with "extreme atrocity or cruelty" can never be paroled.

Yet paradoxically, a senseless murder or unprovoked assault may betray a mind so deranged that a defendant cannot be held responsible for his acts. On Thanksgiving Day, 1980, a middle-aged woman in Reno, Nevada, drove her car up onto busy sidewalks, running down and killing six people she didn't know. Earlier that same year a Boston man wielded a meat cleaver on motorists caught in a traffic jam. Insane crimes are a disturbingly regular feature of the evening news.

Even primitive societies identify certain individuals as mentally incompetent, not to be held responsible for deviant behavior. In the civilized world, criminal courts have long recognized the injustice of punishing those who cannot understand the law, as well as the futility of trying to deter those who cannot control their actions. Some categories of legal incompetence have been easy to define. Courts have had little difficulty recognizing individuals who are so simple-minded they must be excused from criminal punishment. Likewise, legislatures have established specific ages that determine whether an offender is to be tried and sentenced as a juvenile or an adult. Occasionally there is public pressure to deny immunity in marginal cases — to try a fifteen-year-old murderer as an adult, for example — and there may be mild disagreement over just where to set the boundaries of responsibility; but no one doubts that, questions of degree aside, such defendants can and should be identified and given special consideration.

By contrast, the legal system has never found a satisfactory process to distinguish insane defendants from those who are merely evil, or the truly deranged from the impostors. Moreover, general willingness to excuse those who cannot control their behavior or understand the law has been countered by a fear of letting people get away with murder. This backlash has been felt not only in particular cases — an Illinois jury convicted John Wayne Gacy of the monstrously sick crime of killing thirty-three boys and young men, for example — but in debates over broader policy. There have been proposals in state assemblies, including New York's, to abolish the insanity defense outright.

The insanity plea itself rests on a tangle of contradictions. A defendant who invokes insanity to avoid jail does so at the price of imposing a stigma on himself, and may risk longer confinement in a different but equally unpleasant institution. In some instances the insanity defense is more readily accepted for lesser crimes than for serious offenses, but often the reverse is true. One who claims insanity often admits not only his crime but his uncontrollable propensity to commit it again — and on this basis argues that he should be absolved of guilt. Even moderate voices agree that the defense needs scrutiny and perhaps revision.

Growing controversy about the insanity defense has paralleled increased apprehension about crime in general. Each year more than a million violent crimes are committed in the United States—murders, muggings, rapes, family violence. Many of these acts can be attributed to malice or greed, but a great many others seem to be the work of twisted minds. Recent attacks on famous people, attacks involving motives and behavior so bizarre that they can only be seen as madness, have put the issue of criminal insanity on the front page.

Mark Chapman, who for years had identified himself with John Lennon, sold all his belongings, traveled from Hawaii to New York, and lurked around the ex-Beatle's home for more than a week—even taking care to obtain Lennon's autograph—before killing him. Chapman had been in a mental institution and twice had attempted suicide. After the arrest a police official quoted him as saying, "Most of me didn't want to do it, but a little of me did. I couldn't help myself."

John Hinckley, who tried to assassinate President Reagan, had an equally troubled past. Family friends had seen the once-affable young man become reclusive and hostile. In 1980 he had been caught trying to carry guns and ammunition aboard an airplane; apparently he had been stalking President Carter during the election campaign. After his arrest for the Reagan shooting, investigators discovered letters indicating that Hinckley intended to avenge an imagined presidential snub of Jodie Foster. He had never met the teen-age actress, but thought his gesture would win her favor.

Though we see ours as an age peculiarly plagued by inexplicable violence, the problem of understanding criminal insanity is long-standing. A century ago Charles Guiteau was hanged for the assassination of President James Garfield in the teeth of evidence that by present standards he was mad as a hatter. Guiteau had a long history of strange schemes and erratic behavior. "Removal" of the president, as he termed it, was an unfortunate necessity, compelled by direct instruction from God. Guiteau irrationally expected adulation from the same public that had just elected Garfield; he believed that newly elevated President Chester Arthur was bound to reward his benefactor.

Guiteau's lawyers' attempt to prove insanity was seemingly

bolstered by his frequent outbursts during the trial, but the medical establishment and the court would have none of it. Guiteau (like Chapman and Hinckley years later) had selected his target, bought his gun, and tracked his victim before the shooting. The prosecution successfully contended that such careful deliberation was utterly inconsistent with the prevailing conception of criminal insanity: that is, some sort of emotionally explosive event, the result of an irresistible impulse. Guiteau was, it was widely agreed, simulating insanity. Even today history books remember him as a "disappointed office seeker" (hence the unwitting author of civil-service reform) rather than as a lunatic.

In retrospect it is easy to dismiss nineteenth-century conceptions of mental illness as unenlightened, and the law on which they were based as harsh. Yet while medical knowledge of the mind has become more sophisticated, the problem of applying the insanity defense has, if anything, grown more difficult. During most of the last century insanity was thought to be caused by some sort of physical lesion, usually, but not always, located in the brain itself. Except in obvious instances of raving mania, lawyers undertaking an insanity defense were constrained to prove the physical ailment from which their clients' mental incapacity stemmed.

Freudian theory ultimately shifted the focus in criminal trials from organic to emotional and environmental explanations of insane behavior. Still, the public—in particular, the typical jury member—has never fully embraced psychiatry. Moreover, psychiatry itself has failed to present a united front, even on "simple" questions of sanity and insanity. Twenty-five years ago Supreme Court Justice Felix Frankfurter declared that "the only certain thing that can be said about the present state of knowledge regarding mental disease is that science has not reached the finality of judgment." Notwithstanding recent advances, insanity trials still often degenerate into battles between experts, in which competing psychiatric theories are in the dock with the defendant.

Disputes within the medical profession over the nature of

mental illness have amplified the controversy over the insanity defense. The lack of medical consensus has also given judges and juries a freer hand to follow their own instincts—and biases. A jury may convict a mass murderer, even if it privately recognizes he is crazy, in order to ensure that he will serve a long prison sentence and not be sent to a mental institution where he may soon be pronounced "cured" and be released. In other circumstances, a jury may use an insanity verdict to exonerate a perfectly normal person from guilt for a mercy killing or a crime of passion.

The dominance of psychogenic explanations of insanity is now being challenged, but the new medical theories are likely to raise still more legal problems. Neurologists and pharmacologists have discovered physical triggers for behavior that traditional psychoanalysts had attributed to emotional disturbances. Daily doses of lithium allow some manic-depressives to lead normal lives. Schizophrenia and other psychoses often can be tempered by antipsychotic drugs. Some researchers are convinced that if chemicals can be used to control mental disease, then faulty brain chemistry must be at the core of criminal insanity. Indeed, in late 1981 researchers at the University of Chicago's Laboratory of Biological Psychiatry announced the discovery of a simple blood test that may allow doctors not only to diagnose clinical depression (the most prevalent mental illness), but also to identify people who are most likely to develop it.

The biochemistry of mental illness can raise troublesome legal issues. The woman who was arrested for running down pedestrians in Reno was immediately committed to a mental hospital. Physicians there prescribed antipsychotic drugs so that she would be competent to stand trial, but she refused to take them. After a series of legal battles, the Nevada Supreme Court ruled that she had to accept the drug treatment.

Even the most ardent proponents of organic causes of abnormal behavior concede that we are many years from seeing insanity conclusively proved by brain scans and blood tests; yet there already have been some famous cases in which physical and chemical disorders have been implicated in violent crime. Charles Whitman, the "Texas Tower sniper" who killed a dozen people and wounded thirty-three others before he himself was shot by police, had earlier sought help from a university psychiatrist. Whitman confessed a terrible urge to climb a tall tower and start shooting. The psychiatrist tried to address the problem through a traditional Freudian inquiry into his patient's feelings about his parents. After the murders, however, an autopsy on Whitman revealed a malignant brain tumor that may have precipitated his outburst. Melvin Belli unsuccessfully tried to develop similar evidence in preparing to defend Jack Ruby, the man who shot Kennedy assassin Lee Harvey Oswald.

More recently, lawyers defending Dan White—the former San Francisco supervisor who killed Mayor George Moscone and Supervisor Harvey Milk—presented expert testimony that the witness had been depressed and that his mental condition had been exacerbated by a blood-sugar abnormality. The blood problem was related, in turn, to White's junk-food diet. The press mocked the argument as the "Twinkie defense," but the court apparently gave it more respect, finding that White suffered from diminished mental capacity, and sentenced him to only a few years in jail for the double homicide.

Whether involving conventional psychiatric testimony or novel organic evidence, celebrated crimes are seldom good illustrations of the insanity defense and its implications. Where the victim is famous or the criminal act horrendous, as in the case of mass murders, the trial inevitably becomes so sensationalized that the subtle issues inherent in determining insanity and responsibility are overshadowed. For example, beyond the question of whether Madeira School headmistress Jean Harris acted out of madness or simple jealousy is the broader matter of whether our courts are competent to make such judgments. Predictably, the trial of the killer of Scarsdale-diet doctor Herman Tarnower was publicized as either a real-life soap opera or a feminist psychodrama, but certainly not as a test of our medical and legal institutions.

Moreover, the public cry for retribution in famous cases may be so strong that it distorts the process and the outcome. The same society that in hindsight might regard the hanging of Guiteau as barbaric did not blink at the conviction of Arthur Bremer, the man who shot George Wallace in 1972, even though the two assassins—and their crimes—seem indistinguishable. Bremer had tracked a number of presidential candidates before settling on Wallace. In his diary he said that when he pulled the trigger, he wanted to ask, "A penny for your thoughts." In an era when the public was reeling from a series of assassinations, however, Bremer, no matter how crazy, could not expect to find refuge in the insanity defense.

For every Bremer, Chapman, and Hinckley, there are tens of thousands of nameless defendants whose violent crimes may— or may not—be triggered by mental illness. Because their victims are ordinary people and because their crimes are all too common, such defendants are for the most part tried and judged in obscurity. It is the sum of these cases, however, that defines the law of criminal insanity: who shall be jailed, who shall be hospitalized, and who shall be set free.

The easy cases are those in which the motives and mental state of the accused are clear. At one extreme are those violent crimes whose very circumstances appear to explain themselves: for instance, the shooting of a bank guard in the midst of a robbery. At the other are acts so strange they can only be the product of twisted minds. But between these poles are countless instances of violence in which the causes are ambiguous. That the words *angry* and *mad* are often used interchangeably reflects the blurry line between these two emotional states, yet one results in criminal culpability and the other in exoneration.

Criminal trials are, in part, attempts to reconstruct the past. This is particularly so when insanity is at issue, for then it is not enough to establish what happened; it is also necessary to determine why. Assessing a person's present mental state is hard enough, but divining a defendant's psyche at the time of a crime, months or even years earlier, is that much more difficult. When a defendant claims temporary insanity, the issue is quite literally ephemeral. Finally, even when the defendant can establish that he did suffer from a mental disease or defect, the court must still determine whether that condition precipitated the crime.

As medical theories of mental disease have become increasingly technical, some legal scholars have advocated removing the insanity question from the province of lay judges and juries, and putting it in the hands of specialized tribunals. Jurors, they fear, may resist psychiatric doctrine and be overwhelmed by biochemical testimony. Some juries may ignore or reject such evidence and convict people who should not be held accountable for their actions. Other juries, of course, may err in the opposite direction and blindly rubber-stamp an expert's conclusion without testing its basis. A defendant's fate may turn disproportionately on the nature and mood of the jury he happens to draw. Yet if there is a price to be paid when the ultimate diagnosis of insanity is made by untutored people, there may also be significant costs in deciding such cases outside the normal legal process. The judicial system is designed not merely to protect the rights of the accused but also to represent the interests of society. In cases where personal liberty and public safety are in precarious balance, the judge and jury have an essential role.

Coupled with the question of who should decide insanity is the issue of whether the traditional adversary process helps or hinders the inquiry. Defense lawyers and prosecutors have responsibility to represent their clients zealously, not necessarily to assist the fact finder in a quest for truth. The formal rules of evidence that bind the courtroom lawyer are different from the scientific procedures that guide the physician and researcher who investigate a patient's mental condition.

These issues are so broad that it is easy to see them only as abstractions; yet judges and juries daily must sort out conflicting evidence and accommodate competing social values. Though no single insanity case should be taken as a conclusive test of the adequacy of our legal and medical institutions, a detailed examination of one trial can reveal in concrete terms the practices and proclivities of the lawyers and doctors who seek to define and explain criminal violence.

# 2. Violence

THE SUPERIOR COURTHOUSE in New Bedford, Massachusetts, was built in 1830, two decades before Herman Melville described Ishmael's voyage from that city. Today newer buildings obscure the view of the harbor, but a breeze from the sea still puts a raw edge on a spring morning.

The courtroom itself is on the second floor, up a dark flight of stairs. The pale-blue paint on the walls is starting to peel and the handsome benches for spectators deserve refinishing, but the general neglect has meant that much of the room's remarkable past has been undisturbed. Gas light fixtures (which replaced the original whale-oil lamps) are still on the wall. Portraits of early lawyers and judges such as Timothy Coffin, Jeremiah Eliot, John Clifford, and Hosea Knowlton ring the front of the room. In an alcove high above the judge's bench is a classical bust—possibly of Caesar—that even the oldest court employees cannot identify, but that has kept its place through seniority. The vaulted room with its brass chandeliers looks much as it did in 1893 when Knowlton prosecuted Lizzie Borden there for the ax murder of her father and stepmother. Worldwide interest in the Borden case was so intense that all the spectator seats in the courtroom were taken by the press. Crowds milled outside to catch secondhand reports of the trial. Today the spectator benches are mostly empty, even when bloody crimes are being tried.

For Frank O'Boy the New Bedford courthouse had by 1976 long been familiar territory. As an assistant district attorney for three years and a private practitioner in nearby Taunton for nine years before that, he had tried dozens of cases in the old courtroom. He doubted that *Commonwealth v. Decker* would make his reputation or change his professional life—by April 5, 1976, the case was old news, if it was news at all—yet the case clearly demanded more than routine attention. In the nearly two years since his arrest, the defendant had waived his right to a speedy trial four separate times so that his lawyer, David Roseman, could construct a novel defense.

After the preliminary motions were taken care of, O'Boy was ready to begin the prosecution. "I just want to state that the first witness, Miss Sussman,* is still suffering some effects of this," he told the court. "May she be allowed to sit down?" Witnesses are usually required to stand on a small wooden platform with a handrail in front, but, with the assent of Judge Thomas Dwyer, a bailiff produced a chair for the slim seventeen-year-old high-school student. Sometimes such a request is a prosecutor's gambit to impress upon a judge the seriousness of the victim's injuries, but in this instance O'Boy was truly concerned about how well his witness would be able to stand up to the physical and emotional strain of testifying. Her hair was still short; her head had been shaved for the surgery that had saved her life. Whenever O'Boy had seen her—at the probable-cause hearings, at pretrial interviews—Sussman had been accompanied by the school psychologist who now sat by himself in the spectator section. O'Boy knew that his witness was terrified to be in the same room with the man who had attacked her.

"Will you tell the court your name, please?" he asked.

"My name is Gail Sussman."

David Roseman, seated at the defense table directly opposite the witness, said he could not hear. Judge Dwyer told the young

---

*The names of the two victims and the defendant have been changed.

woman to speak up. "We want you to feel good. There is no need to be nervous. Answer these questions as best you can. Anytime you don't feel good, raise your hand. One of the things you have got to do," the judge added, "is to talk so loud that everybody in the back row has to hear you. A girl with your voice, you really have to yell."

In fact there was no one in the back row. The defendant had waived his right to a jury, so the box to Sussman's left was empty. Decker sat alone in the dock. Behind him were his father and his physician. A few lawyers drifted in and out, intent on other matters. The area right around the witness stand, however, was crowded. The judge's bench was just to Sussman's right, and the stenographer sat poised immediately in front of her. O'Boy moved away from his table to encourage Sussman to talk louder. Methodically he had her explain that she lived in Seekonk—a town on the Rhode Island border—and that on July 17, 1974, she was fifteen and had just finished her sophomore year at the local high school. That evening she and Deborah Sharp, a schoolmate, had hitchhiked to another friend's house. The friend wasn't home, so with little to do they headed for Slater's Park in nearby Pawtucket. They thought about walking, she said, but they decided to thumb another ride.

Sussman managed to maintain her composure during the preliminary questioning, but when O'Boy asked if she had seen a car go by, her voice faltered. Prodded by the prosecutor and the judge to speak up, she testified that a little after 7:00 P.M. they had been passed by a smallish, light-colored convertible with the rear window taped up. "It went by the opposite way of us first, and then it came back towards us. Then it went around again, and then it came back and picked us up." The car stopped in front of them, Sussman said, and the driver reached over to open the passenger door to let them in.

"Do you see the driver of that car in the courtroom today?" asked O'Boy.

"Yes, I do."

"Will you point out to his Honor the driver of that car?"

Sussman raised her hand and pointed at a tall, well-built young man, about twenty-three, with a blond mustache, who was sitting motionless in the prisoner's dock. "He's sitting over there with a brown jacket and brown tie," she said. O'Boy asked that the record reflect that she had pointed out the defendant, Charles Decker. That Decker was well dressed set him apart from many defendants who appear in criminal court, but his good clothes did not hide the rugged physique of a man used to hard labor. Though he was charged with a brutal crime, Decker's Teutonic features were set in an impassive mask, concealing whatever feelings he had about Gail Sussman and the events she was about to describe. As a matter of routine, a court officer was seated near the prisoner.

O'Boy had his witness go on to explain how she and her friend had introduced themselves as they climbed into the defendant's car. Deborah sat in back and Gail took the passenger seat. She caught Charles's first name, but could only remember the first letter of his surname. He passed them a bottle of beer. After they each took a drink, he finished it himself. The girls decided that they did not really care about going to the park, so Charles drove up the road a mile or so to Oscar's Food Land to get cigarettes and more beer. Oscar's is a small, one-story, flat-roofed building that sits almost at the edge of the street. The name of the store hangs under a large Budweiser sign.

O'Boy asked Sussman whether having listened to the defendant and having seen him walk in and out of the store, she was able to judge his sobriety. "Yes," Sussman answered. "He wasn't loaded and he wasn't drunk or anything."

Sussman explained that for the next forty-five minutes Charles, Deborah, and she had cruised the roads of Seekonk and neighboring Rehoboth. The commercial strip, with its fast-food places and dry-cleaning stores, gave way to woods and fields. The area near the state line is more rural than suburban. It was still early summer, and the sun had not set. Charles and the girls shared the beers and small talk. O'Boy asked Sussman if she could remember what was said, but she could not. The lawyer continued, "Could you tell us something as to the tone of voice he used during whatever the conversation was you had?"

"The same, you know, like a nice guy. He didn't seem mean or anything."

"Upset?" asked the prosecutor.

"He didn't seem to be upset about anything," she answered.

According to Sussman, Charles said that he had to go home for a few minutes. He was married, he admitted, and he had to check in, but he promised that if they wanted to go riding around, he would come back and pick them up. The girls got out near the Lighthouse, a seafood place, to wait. In an earlier time the restaurant might have been called a roadhouse—cars can almost park under the eaves. The building is cluttered with signs advertising littlenecks, clam cakes, hot dogs, lobsters, and Lighthouse Computer Software. In ten or fifteen minutes Charles reappeared. He had brought another six-pack of beer and some marijuana.

While O'Boy was eliciting Sussman's testimony, David Roseman, at the defense table, was quietly attentive. He interrupted only to ask that the witness speak up or to clarify which of the photographs she identified were being formally offered as evidence. Roseman had not been retained until several months after Charles's arrest, so he had not heard Sussman tell her story at the probable-cause hearing. Sitting behind Roseman were Charles's father, Nicholas Decker, and his father's long-time friend and associate, Dr. Mark Altschule. Both men had been at the first hearing. They felt that even though the young woman was the prosecution's chief witness, much of her testimony, far from condemning Charles, was evidence in itself that he had been insane. They listened carefully as the girl detailed Charles's peculiar behavior on that summer night nearly two years earlier.

O'Boy had Sussman continue her account, step by step. She explained that after Charles picked them up the second time, he let her drive. O'Boy asked where the defendant sat. "I think he sat on the transmission," she answered. O'Boy had the witness identify a photograph of the inside of the car. It had bucket seats and two doors. Deborah sat on the passenger side.

O'Boy asked where she drove. "I don't know," Sussman said. "It was just down Mason Street, there's—I think there's a stop sign at the end of it or something, and I had to stop fast—you know, short. And when I stopped, when I put the brake on, this hammer slid out from under the seat."

"What?" asked Judge Dwyer.

"A sledgehammer slid out from underneath the driver's seat."

O'Boy had Sussman stand up and point on the photograph to show where she saw the hammer appear. He asked her to describe the hammer, and she held her hands apart to indicate the size. "It's a short handle." O'Boy walked back to his table and picked up a four-pound stonemason's hammer, the sort used to split bricks and paving blocks. "Showing you an object here, can you identify that, Gail?"

"Yes."

"Could you tell his Honor what that is?"

"That's the hammer he hit us with."

*

Judge Dwyer recessed the trial for lunch. That afternoon O'Boy had Sussman resume her testimony. She explained that she had continued to drive the car. There was no reason at that point for Deborah or her to be concerned about the hammer. Charles produced a bag of marijuana (Roseman made a perfunctory objection that she was not qualified to identify the substance), rolled a joint and passed it around. At some point—Sussman was not sure just where—they were stopped by a police car. Given the open beer, marijuana, and an underage driver, there could have been problems. "Charles got out and he came back after a couple of minutes, and Debbie asked him what was going on. And he said, 'You know, the cop just stopped us because one of the lights was out.'" Sussman added, "He told Deb and me that he told the cop that he was teaching his girl friend to drive."

Charles climbed in on the driver's side and Gail slid over to the transmission, next to Deborah in the passenger's seat. According to Sussman, Charles "seemed a little mad" and did not say much as he drove along back roads in Rehoboth, roads that were familiar to her from cruising with friends. Charles pulled on to Brook Street, swung the car around, and parked just off the pavement. Though the road was not isolated, he told the girls he had to go to urinate.

O'Boy asked Sussman what she and Deborah did during the

one or two minutes Charles was gone. "Well, when he was outside," she answered, "Debbie and I decided we wanted to go home because it was getting dark."

"When he came back did you or Deborah say anything to him?"

"Yes. We asked him if he could bring us up to Route 6 or around there so we could get home."

O'Boy continued. "What, if anything, did he say or do?"

"He didn't say anything." Sussman explained that the three sat silently in the dark, Charles rubbing his hands on his legs.

"Did something happen?" asked O'Boy.

"Yes."

"Will you tell his Honor what happened?"

"Well, we asked him, and he didn't say anything. Then all of a sudden he just hit me with the hammer."

"Where did he hit you, Gail?"

"On my head."

"How many times?"

"I don't know," she said.

"What happened to you as a result?"

"I had a fractured skull."

David Roseman started to interrupt. O'Boy, anticipating defense counsel's objection that no foundation had been laid for the statement, acknowledged, "I was getting ahead..."

Roseman spoke up: "I move to strike."

Judge Dwyer, without waiting for argument on the point, ruled, "It may be stricken." O'Boy rephrased his question for Sussman: "Were you rendered unconscious at that time?"

"Not really unconscious. I just like blacked out for a second."

"When you came to where were you?"

"I was still in the car."

"And where was he?" asked O'Boy. "That is, the defendant— Decker?"

"When I came to, Debbie was trying to get out on the passenger's side, and Charles ran around the car. I guess he still had the hammer in his hand. He knocked Debbie down and was hitting her."

"Where was Debbie knocked down with him hitting her?"

"She was trying to get out of the car."

O'Boy wanted a precise description of the scene. "Was she still in the car?"

"She was half in it."

"Where was he?"

"He was outside," Sussman answered.

"Did you observe anything in his hand?"

"Well, I couldn't really say that, but it looked like that. It was really in the dark."

David Roseman spoke up. "I couldn't get that."

Judge Dwyer had the stenographer read Sussman's last answer, and then O'Boy continued his questioning. "What happened to Debbie?"

"He was hitting her, and he picked her up and put her in the car with her head on the floor and her feet backwards to how you usually sit in the car."

"In other words," said O'Boy, "her head was on the floor and her back was against the seat?"

"Yes."

"Her feet were in the air?"

"Yes."

"Did you observe anything about her?" asked O'Boy.

"Yes. I thought she was dead because she wasn't breathing."

"Did you notice anything about her head?"

"I couldn't see it," Sussman said. "It was down on the floor."

O'Boy moved back to the prosecutor's table, picked up an object, and continued his questioning. "If I may, you say that he struck you across the head?" Sussman nodded yes.

"Did you see what he struck you with?"

Sussman hesitated. O'Boy persisted. "Will you answer that?"

"Yes, I did."

Sussman was becoming increasingly anxious, but O'Boy bore in on his own witness. "What did he hit you with?"

"That hammer," she answered. "Will you put it down please. It's making me nervous."

O'Boy held the hammer right in front of her. "Showing you Commonwealth Exhibit A for identification, you identify this as what he had in his hand when he hit you in the head in the car?"

"Does she know?" Roseman interjected.

"She already identified this," noted the judge.

O'Boy wanted to leave no doubt. "Does that look like the hammer?"

"Yes," Sussman answered, "it does."

The hammer was marked and accepted as a formal exhibit for the Commonwealth, and O'Boy went on with his examination. "What, if anything, did you or Deborah say while he was hitting you and when he was hitting her?"

"I screamed. I know that," Sussman said. "Then after he put Deb back in the car, you know, I felt her stomach to see if she was breathing," she added. Sussman found no sign of life. "I thought he killed her." She was both terrified and enraged. "You've killed my best friend," she cried. O'Boy asked what happened next. "He was really mad that I said that, I guess, and he started to choke me."

"Where were you at this time?"

"I was still in the middle."

"Where was he?"

Sussman explained that Charles had gotten back in the car, on the driver's side. O'Boy asked, "As he started to choke you, will you describe what he did?"

"Well, he just put his hands on me. Like he started choking me and pushing my head."

"What did you say and what did you do?"

"I tried to kick him and scratch him and punch him and everything, so he wouldn't do it, and I tried to choke him back," Sussman said.

"Did he say anything?" asked O'Boy.

"I don't remember him saying anything, but when I was trying to choke him back he hurt me and it hurt. I'm pretty sure I ripped his T-shirt."

"What else did he say or do?"

"Nothing."

"At some time did he cease trying to choke you?" asked the prosecutor.

"Well, when he was trying to choke me I figured maybe if I

pretend I'm dead maybe he won't try to hurt me anymore. And I tried that for a couple of seconds. It didn't work. He kept choking me hard, and I don't know, he just stopped."

"What happened then?"

"He just started the car and he drove, and I was just sitting there trying to figure out what was going on. And he didn't say anything."

"Did you say anything while he was driving along after this incident?" asked O'Boy.

"I don't remember saying anything."

"What did you observe as to the condition of Deborah?"

"She didn't look too good."

"Conscious or unconscious?"

"No, she was unconscious."

Sussman testified that she knew they were somewhere in Rehoboth but that she was unfamiliar with the road. The area was more remote than the place where they first parked. O'Boy asked, "Did he stop at some other place?"

"He drove around," she answered, "and then he went down this bumpy road that was dirty and all bumpy. And it had these little raggedy bush tree things that you see in the cowboy movies."

"Something like mesquite?" O'Boy suggested.

"Yes, those kinds of things." Sussman added, "And he just stopped the car, and he said, 'Get out.'"

Charles walked around the car to the passenger side and got Deborah out. Sussman was not sure, but she thought he dropped her friend on the ground. Sussman herself, though scared and upset, started to leave the car on her own. "I felt my head and it was all mushy. I put my hand in the car and it was all bloody and everything." As she got out she was frightened to see that Charles was holding a large rock, perhaps a foot long. "It was smooth, though," she remembered. "It wasn't bumpy." Charles hurled the rock at her.

"Did it strike you?" O'Boy asked.

"I think it did."

"Do you know where it struck you?"

"If it hit me, it hit me in the head," Sussman said. Charles had left Deborah sprawled on the ground and was concentrating on Gail. He picked up another rock, smaller than the first but more jagged, and threw it at her.

O'Boy had to interrupt Sussman's testimony as the wail of a passing police car was drowning out her voice. After it went by, O'Boy asked what happened next.

"I don't know," Sussman answered. "For some reason I was thinking of football, and I just grabbed the rock. And I guess I fell on the ground with it, when you play tackle."

Gail had stumbled around to the driver's side of the car. Charles followed and lifted her up. He wrestled the rock away from her, threw it again, but missed. Then he went back to the passenger side where Deborah lay. As Charles moved, Gail tried to circle the car, keeping it between him and her. "I was walking around it and trying to calm him down."

"What were you saying?" asked O'Boy. "What was he saying, if anything?"

"Well, I remember saying that just to leave us here where we were, and, you know, we wouldn't tell anybody what he did. And he said, 'No, you're going to tell,' you know. I said, 'No, we are not going to tell.'"

O'Boy asked how many times she had said this. Sussman was not sure, but thought it was "probably a lot." O'Boy asked her to describe how Charles seemed at that time.

"Well," said Sussman, "before I started talking to him and trying to calm him down, like he told me to unbutton my shirt and take it off, and I said no."

"And did he say anything when you said no?"

"I can't remember him saying anything."

"How many times did he ask you to take your shirt off?" said O'Boy.

"He asked me two times."

"What did you say?"

"I said no both times."

"Where were you in relation to the car while this conversation was going on?"

"We were on opposite sides of the car."

"Were you moving around the car?"

"Yes."

"At some time did you touch the antenna, if you remember?"

"I don't know if I really touched the car because I couldn't see so good," said Sussman.

"Would you tell us why you couldn't see real good?" asked O'Boy.

"Because my head was all mushy."

"Did you feel something?"

"Yes, a lot of mush, blood."

"At some time did he say something to you further?"

"I don't understand," said Sussman.

O'Boy elaborated. "After he asked you to take your blouse off and you refused, you told him you wouldn't tell anybody if he'd leave you there?"

"Oh, yes. Well, he just sort of after...I don't know. I was talking to him, trying to calm him down — like an hysterical kid. You try to calm a little kid down."

David Roseman had been paying careful attention, but he quickly interrupted, saying "I don't get it." The court stenographer read Sussman's statement back word for word. Roseman had no objection to either the question or the answer.

O'Boy continued his examination. "You said he was hysterical or he was talking..."

"Like I was talking to one — really upset."

"Could you describe what you observed about his emotional state at that time?" Sussman proceeded to describe how Charles's violent outburst abated almost as suddenly as it had erupted: "After I was talking to him he seemed like...I don't know, he just calmed down like a little kid."

"Before he calmed down, what did you observe?" inquired O'Boy.

"He seemed real mad. I don't know, really strange."

"At some time did he say something to you about taking you someplace?"

"After he calmed down a little, he just eased up, and he was just calm. And he said"—Sussman paused—"he said, 'Get back in the car and I'll bring you some place where there's a light on so somebody can help you.'" Gail was leery. "I don't believe you," she told him. "How do I know you're not going to beat us up any more?" Charles had exploded twice, so his promise not to hurt them seemed worthless. Still Gail was not sure where she was. There was no place in sight to get help. She knew that she and Deborah desperately needed a doctor.

Charles tried to help the girls back into the car, Sussman testified, but she was not sure whether she had let him. She was certain that she put Deborah in front. She did not want her friend trapped in the back seat of a two-door car. "I kept my arm around her, and usually I lock the car door but I didn't. And I kept my other hand on the door-opener thing, so that if he tried anything else I figured I could jump out, me and Deb."

O'Boy asked what Deborah's face looked like. "It was all bloody," Sussman explained, "like caked mud and junk. He started the car, and he drove out of that deserted-like place. And then Debbie woke up for a minute and looked at me. And she told me that I looked terrible. And then he just drove us over to Santos' because there was a light on. He said, 'There's a light on and they'll help you.'"

Sussman was unable to remember the roads they took to Santos' Market or how long the trip lasted. O'Boy asked what happened when they reached the store.

"He said, 'You can get out here. There's a light on and somebody will help you,' And he went around, got out of the car, stopped the car, and went around. And then he opened the door and tried to help me out, but I didn't want him to touch me."

"Did you say anything to him?" asked O'Boy.

"No. I just shook his arm off."

"What did you do?"

"I just got out, helped Debbie out, and he got back in and took off real fast."

O'Boy showed Sussman a photograph of Santos' Market, a white shingled building at the intersection of two rural roads.

She pointed to the spot in the parking area, just beyond a tree, where Charles had dropped them off. O'Boy asked what they had done after the defendant left.

"Well, Debbie was still unconscious. I had to help her up the lawn. The lawn is really big, and we finally got up there, up to the steps, and Debbie got sick and she passed out. And I was knocking on the door, and then Mrs. Santos came to the door."

"Did the police arrive some time later?"

"It seemed like I was talking to her, and I told her...I think I told her my name and to call the police. And then they came. They were there in three seconds, it seemed."

An ambulance was called, and Deborah and Gail were first taken to Union Hospital in Fall River, Massachusetts, but because of the seriousness of their head injuries they were quickly moved to Rhode Island Hospital in Providence. Both underwent brain surgery early the next morning.

*

Charles Decker had pleaded not guilty to two counts of attempted murder, but Frank O'Boy was satisfied that his principal witness had established a very strong case. In fact, from the outset O'Boy had enough confidence in Sussman that he did not plan on calling Deborah Sharp, the other victim, to testify. (At the time of the trial she happened to be hospitalized for minor surgery unrelated to Decker's attacks; O'Boy could have gotten a postponement for the asking.) During O'Boy's opening, Judge Dwyer had interrupted to ask, "Why is this case going to trial without one of the victims?" The judge, who had been a prominent criminal lawyer before his appointment to the bench, appeared to be second-guessing the prosecutor. O'Boy stated that Sharp would add nothing to what Sussman could testify. Even though Sharp was unconscious after the first attack, however, she could have corroborated Gail's account of the earlier events. "It's your case," said the judge.

Sussman's testimony confirmed O'Boy's decision. In the courtroom, she pointed out Charles without hesitation, and in her answers she consistently referred to him by name. She identified his hammer as the weapon used in the first assault.

Later O'Boy had her identify a torn T-shirt as the one she had ripped in her struggle with Charles.

A few portions of her testimony were unclear—she seemed confused about whether Deborah had been conscious when they arrived at Santos' Market—but these were minor points, and, given her injuries, some uncertainty was inevitable. Most important, she had firmly stated that Charles had been completely rational immediately before and right after the attacks. O'Boy had taken care to ask Sussman about her conversation with Charles. He had seemed like a nice guy, she said; not mean or upset. Her assessment was confirmed, at least by implication, by the episode with the police car. After being stopped, Charles apparently had been able to assure the officer that there was not any trouble.

Sussman had also given the prosecutor ammunition to argue that Charles's conduct after the first attack reflected the workings of a rational mind. Though his motive for the hammer attack was a mystery, the second assault, the one with the stones, could easily be seen as a deliberate attempt to finish off his victims to prevent them from identifying him. From Sussman's account, it appeared that Charles had had second thoughts and decided to seek help for the girls in hopes of mitigating his crime. Her statement that he was afraid that they would "tell," and the fact he had sped off, both strongly suggested that his mind was working well enough to distinguish right from wrong.

To establish the Commonwealth's case, O'Boy called just one other witness, Keith Quint of the Rehoboth police. Earlier a map prepared by Quint, showing area roads, Santos' store, and the location of the attacks, had been accepted as an exhibit. Quint, unlike Sussman, stood on the witness stand, but his testimony barely took two minutes. He stated that in the course of investigating the assaults, he had found a car registered to Charles Decker. O'Boy showed him the same photograph that Sussman had identified that morning as a picture of the car that had picked them up. Quint had found the car in deep grass along a main highway, less than a quarter mile from Charles's apartment.

O'Boy asked Quint about one other matter, Sussman's

statement that they had been stopped by a policeman earlier in the evening. "Were you ever able to find the police officer?"

"No," said Quint, "I haven't."

Quint's brief testimony concluded the prosecution's case. The rest of the trial would focus on Roseman's defense—and O'Boy's attempts to shake it. At ten minutes of four Judge Dwyer recessed the trial until ten o'clock the next morning.

\*

O'Boy's examination of Gail Sussman had reconstructed the events of July 17 from shortly after seven in the evening, when Charles Decker had picked up her and her friend, Deborah, to around ten, when he had left them at Santos' store, beaten and bloody. O'Boy had no need to go into what happened afterward. Yet even though the events after ten o'clock were immaterial to proving the crime, they were profoundly important in shaping Charles's defense.

Neither O'Boy nor David Roseman introduced much evidence about Charles's conduct after the attacks, but his father, Nicholas Decker, who had sat through the first day of the trial, knew the story firsthand. He had been at home in Rehoboth that night. His wife was with her ailing mother in Florida, but one of his daughters was staying with him, and his eldest son and his wife were living in a cottage on the property. A little after ten the telephone rang. It was Charles, who lived about a mile away. Charles told his father that he was afraid he might have killed two girls.

Nicholas Decker asked, "What happened?"

"Daddy, I don't know," said Charles. "I went ape. They were teasing me and that's all I know." Decker told his son to come over to the house right away.

When Charles arrived he gave more details. Although his memory was fuzzy and he compressed some events, his basic story was consistent with what Gail Sussman later testified in court. He told his father that he had left his job in Seekonk, where he worked as a landscape gardener, a little after five, and had bought some beer. On his way home he had picked up two teen-age hitchhikers. They cruised the back roads, drank the beer, and, he admitted, smoked some marijuana. Like Sussman he reported that at one point a policeman had pulled them over, but only because one of the taillights was broken.

Charles's story contradicted Sussman's, however, in one potentially significant point. Some time later, according to him, the girls began to tease him sexually. Suddenly he erupted, losing all control over himself. He struck one girl, then the other. Just as suddenly, his rage subsided. Realizing what he had done, he drove the girls, both bleeding profusely from the head, to the parking lot of a store he knew was still open. He lifted them from the car and left them where he was sure they would soon be found. He then went straight home and called his father.

Charles was distraught over what he had done, but Decker tried to convince his son and himself that it was not as serious as Charles feared. Nicholas rationalized that even a minor scalp wound can produce a frightening amount of blood, and Charles had said that he thought both girls were conscious when he left them near the store. Realizing the lateness of the hour, Nicholas told his son, "Look, there's nothing you can do now but go home. Let's sit and wait."

Nicholas Decker was distressed by what Charles had reported, but not altogether surprised. Charles had been a problem since his early teens. The Deckers were an accomplished family — Nicholas himself is a research scientist with a doctorate in endocrinology — but his youngest son's academic record and career had thus far been a disappointing contrast to those of his siblings. An older brother, Greg (after Gregory Pincus, the inventor of the birth-control pill), had excelled in college and graduate school, but Charles Darwin Decker had failed to complete high school. During his late teens he had spent more than a year drifting around the country. He had also had earlier outbursts that led his parents to seek medical and psychiatric advice. There had been several scrapes, as his father called them, culminating in a drunk-driving arrest in which Charles had threatened a policeman.

On the surface Decker tried to remain calm and rational, but inside, he later allowed, he was hysterical. Minutes after Charles left, his distress was amplified when the town ambulance screamed by the house, heading in the direction of the store where his son said he had left the injured girls. Then Charles's sister arrived to tell her father that she had seen his sports car and that it was full of blood. Later that night Charles called, highly agitated, to say that he could not find his stonemason's hammer. Charles was not sure, but he was afraid that he had used the hammer on the girls.

At daybreak Nicholas Decker called the local lawyer who had represented Charles on the traffic incident, to ask if he could learn anything from the police about the events of the previous night. The lawyer called back quickly and said, "I don't know if your son is involved, but the two girls are in the hospital, and the Rehoboth police are chasing all over the place for the perpetrator because they both have fractured skulls and are liable to die."

The lawyer advised Decker that the best thing for Charles to do was to give himself up. First, however, Decker wanted to meet with the lawyer. "I had the boy come over to the house, got him dressed and cleaned up, and we took off in my car," Nicholas Decker said later. The two drove along back roads into Rhode Island, trying to keep out of the way of the police until the attorney had time to reach his Fall River office. Their meeting with the lawyer was brief, but Decker was struck by his son's comment that he wished he had picked up two men who could have beaten him. They decided that Decker would drive Charles back to Rehoboth and surrender him to the police, and the lawyer would follow.

When they went downstairs to the street, Charles exchanged greetings with a young man in casual clothes. As they drove off, he explained to his surprised father that the man, a former schoolmate, was now a Rehoboth policeman. Nicholas Decker, who has a low opinion of lawyers in general, immediately concluded that his attorney had breached their confidence and tipped off the police. (The lawyer, in fact, has a good reputation locally; it may have been necessary for him to talk with the police in order to arrange the surrender.) In any event, Nicholas Decker was perplexed by the officer, whose relaxed manner certainly did not suggest that he regarded Charles as a dangerous criminal.

The Deckers drove the ten or twelve miles from Fall River back to Rehoboth. When Nicholas headed by habit to the site of the old police headquarters (a room above the chief's garage), it was Charles who reminded him that the station had recently been moved. Nicholas Decker explained later, "When we walked in there, I was just nonplused. No one came out and clamped handcuffs on him. The lawyer and the policeman sat down and worked out all the charges. They booked him for two counts of attempted murder, intent to murder, this litany went on. Charlie and I walked around, thinking, talking, and so forth, and here are all these open doors. Naturally I was in a rather upset state, but I couldn't fail to notice this casualness with which this attempted murder was being treated." Decker was also struck by the attitude of his son. Back at the lawyer's office, Charles had seemed to recognize that he had gone "ape," to use his word, or "berserk," to use his father's. The young man was full of remorse.

Because Rehoboth has no jail, the police took him to Taunton, fifteen miles to the northeast. The next morning he was formally arraigned in the Taunton district court. At no point did the police use handcuffs. Nicholas Decker asked a police lieutenant why, given the seriousness of the charges, his son was being treated so casually. The officer answered, "He's a very nice kid."

Decker went home to sort out his thoughts. "I was pretty certain something had gone wrong—there was a high probability that the boy was criminally insane. That was the only thing I could think of." Decker reasoned that "the police recognized the kind of person who could be berserk one moment and calm and collected the next."

Decker's bewilderment at the nonchalance of the local police was rather naive. His principal contact with police had been in New York during Prohibition. A friend of his parents had occasionally served as a translator when foreign police administrators came to study the New York system. As a boy Nicholas had heard the city policemen spin stories about their exploits. (His speech is still laced with terms like *turnkey* and *monkey-shines,* which may have come either from these encounters or from reading pulp novels.) Measured against this background, the demeanor of the Rehoboth police was bound to seem casual. Had they apprehended Charles at the scene of the crime, they probably would not have been so accommodating. Then, too, their courtesy toward Charles may really have been a gesture toward his father, a long-time Rehoboth resident and local figure. If Decker had been correct in his belief that the police recognized Charles as being criminally insane, they undoubtedly would have been much more careful with him.

Still, to Decker the conduct of the police was important. It suggested a reason for Charles's earlier outbursts and his present remorse. No one seemed to think the boy was bad. Nicholas Decker's growing suspicion that Charles was profoundly sick might relieve his son (and himself) of the burden of guilt, but this preliminary diagnosis carried its own frightening implications. Intent on discovering an explanation for Charles's behavior, Nicholas turned to the subject he knew best.

*

After being arraigned on July 19, Charles was sent to Bridgewater State Hospital for twenty days of observation, to determine whether he was competent to stand trial. Competence in this regard merely means an ability to understand the charges that have been made, and the capacity to assist in defending against them. One who is insane at the time of the crime, and continues to be insane, may nonetheless be competent to stand trial. Defendants who are incompetent are almost invariably institutionalized until the time, if ever, they are well enough to be tried. Occasionally competency is in issue, as in the case of Mark Chapman, who killed John Lennon. His attorney wanted to claim insanity (another lawyer had publicly pronounced Chapman "as nutty as a fruitcake"), and initially the defendant complied. Later, however, Chapman reneged, declaring that

God had appeared before him and had told him to change his plea to guilty. In court the lawyer passionately argued that Chapman lacked the competence to take such a grave step, but the trial judge overruled him and accepted Chapman's guilty plea.

Nicholas Decker had no doubt about his son's competence to stand trial. Charles knew what he had done and was able to talk about it rationally. It was possible that during the observation period some deeper problem would be identified, but the senior Decker was not optimistic. The resources of a state facility were bound to be limited, and once his son's competence was obvious, there might be less urgency to probe further. Moreover, whatever examination Charles received was likely to be fundamentally psychiatric.

An endocrinologist himself, Nicholas Decker had a professional, and perhaps personal, distrust of traditional, psychoanalytic theories of insanity. Charles's behavior, recent and past, suggested to Decker a possible neurological problem. He knew that temporal-lobe epilepsy, for example, could trigger aberrational outbursts.

Decker immediately called his old friend and associate, Mark Altschule. Altschule was a physician who taught bedside medicine at Harvard and served as chief medical officer at McLean, the psychiatric branch of Massachusetts General Hospital. A man then in his early seventies, Altschule had always emphasized to his students the integrity of medicine as a healing art, in opposition to the research orientation of many of his counterparts. Decker and others regarded him as a brilliant diagnostician. Indeed, he had consulted Altschule several years before in connection with one of Charles's earlier episodes. Perhaps most important, Altschule had been fighting for decades (against most of his McLean colleagues) for recognition of the physical causes of mental illness. Decker was sure that if his son's problem was medical, then Altschule was the man to identify it, and perhaps prescribe a cure.

When Decker described the assaults, Charles's sudden rage and later remorse, Altschule's first impression was that these outbursts might be symptomatic of an organic problem in the brain. It would take a thorough examination and medical tests, however, to confirm his suspicion. The facilities at Bridgewater were not adequate for the kinds of testing that Altschule had in mind; it would be necessary to get court permission to release Charles to a more sophisticated hospital.

After the twenty days of observation were completed, Charles was brought back to the district court in Taunton for a probable-cause hearing. In one respect the proceeding was a formality. There was no question that the prosecutor would be able to establish the basic elements of the crime and thus have the judge refer the case to a grand jury. Because of the seriousness of the charges, the grand jury would have to issue a formal indictment. But Decker and Altschule hoped to use the hearing to get judicial approval of their proposed examination and tests. Charles's lawyer was primed to argue that the young man quite possibly had a physical problem that needed investigation. Altschule made the trip down from Boston both to lend weight to the legal argument and to hear firsthand the testimony of Gail Sussman, who was the complaining witness.

The court accepted the hospital's report. As expected, the examiners had concluded that Charles was competent to stand trial. The report also stated that he suffered "no significant psychiatric disorder." As Frank O'Boy led Sussman through a brief description of the assaults, Altschule found it significant that her account—particularly her recollection of the suddenness of the attacks—was consistent with Charles's. To the physician, the behavior she described seemed symptomatic of a malfunction related to the primitive limbic system in the brain. The proceedings took an adverse turn for the defense, however, shortly after Charles's lawyer started to raise the possibility of having him tested. According to Nicholas Decker, "The judge cut him off! Didn't want to hear any more. Made up his mind, this character was going over to the New Bedford House of Correction and sit there. None of this business of going to a hospital for medical examinations."

This was a major setback. Without tests, Altschule's suspicions were merely that. They were unlikely to be useful in Charles's eventual trial, and, more important to Nicholas Decker, they were not precise enough to form the basis for treatment. Decker was somewhat consoled when the lawyer told him that he had arranged for Charles to be sent back to Bridgewater instead of the New Bedford prison, but even this small victory proved short-lived. Just after seeing the lawyer drive away ("in his white Cadillac," Decker remembers ruefully), Nicholas learned that his son was being put in a van to go to the jail, not the hospital. He ran back into the courtroom, found O'Boy (who had once done some work for the Rehoboth School Committee when Decker was a member), and persuaded the prosecutor to help him talk to the judge in his chambers.

Decker eventually got to see the judge and hurriedly explained what he wanted. According to Decker, the judge said, "Look, don't talk to me. I have no faith in the damn psychiatrists. The reason I cut your lawyer off so hard this morning is due to the fact that yesterday I had to arraign a man who had been pronounced cured by a whole group of psychiatrists. A policeman saw him in the act of stabbing a woman seventeen times. You want a psychiatrist on this thing, don't get it from me."

Decker told the judge he had exactly the same attitude. He waved a copy of *Newsweek* that had a story about a man who had been released only to murder his mother with a hammer. Decker recalls, "I didn't even have to draw it out. As soon as the judge knew what I was driving at, that I wanted to find out if this boy had a derangement that makes him a criminal — if he is, he's going to stay in jail the rest of his life, he'll get no help from me — but if it's a disease and curable, then..." The judge ordered a court officer, "Get that boy out of the wagon. Now."

*

Nicholas Decker had succeeded, at least in part, where the lawyer had failed. Bridgewater State Hospital is no resort (it was the setting for *Titicut Follies,* Frederick Wiseman's documentary on the inhumanity of mental institutions), but at least it was a better place for Charles, particularly if he was sick. But beyond that Decker felt stymied. His son stood charged with two counts of attempted murder. An eminent physician was ready to perform tests, but the court would not allow them. Bailing Charles out would get him into a laboratory, but it would also put him back on the streets before anyone had a clear idea of the likelihood of his being violent again. Decker felt that the two alternatives offered by the legal system—continued incarceration with no testing, or complete release on bond—were both unacceptable. He had lost what little confidence he had in his lawyer. It was time to find another.

# 3. Law

DAVID ROSEMAN BELIEVES that a trial lawyer must practice a hard eye. "You have to look skeptically at any case that comes to your desk. People generally have a capacity to deceive themselves." Clients caught up in their own causes can embellish favorable facts and overlook contrary ones.

Roseman was intrigued with the Decker case from the start — not just with Nicholas Decker's description of the circumstances but also with the story the prosecution's chief witness, Gail Sussman, told at the probable-cause hearing. According to Roseman, "If you just take the account of the girl, the victim, and put the facts down on a piece of paper, they're very peculiar." Roseman ticks off the significant elements: "She testified that he wasn't drunk. There was no antecedent provocation. There was no suggestion of sex before the act. There was this alleged violent explosion, then a return to normal remorseful behavior. Charles made sure the girls were left at a place where they could be helped." To the lawyer, the facts themselves seemed like evidence of an unsound mind.

Roseman first heard the story from Charles's father in early October, more than three months after the attacks. Nicholas Decker, frustrated by his inability to get court permission to have his son medically tested, had turned to a Boston law firm he had used many years earlier in a real-estate suit. His old lawyer had retired, so Decker was sent down the hall to meet Roseman.

David Roseman hardly fits the stereotype of the flamboyant criminal-defense lawyer. His suits are conservative, his manner decidedly subdued, and his downtown Boston office could easily be that of a senior vice-president of a bank. At five-thirty or six each day, when many of the city's trial lawyers retire to the bar at Maison Robert, Roseman heads home to run his customary three miles. His colleagues do mostly corporate and commercial work, but Roseman has been in criminal courts both as defense counsel and as prosecutor. From 1966 to 1969 he was an Assistant United States Attorney handling both civil and criminal matters. A Kennedy Democrat, Roseman left the government after Richard Nixon's election and went back to private practice, principally to do civil litigation. When criminal cases occasionally do come to his firm, they usually are referred to him.

Nicholas Decker explained his son's problem to Roseman in great detail, describing not only the assaults and the initial court proceedings but also Charles's earlier outbursts. He stressed Dr. Altschule's suspicion that Charles suffered from some sort of metabolic abnormality in the brain, perhaps triggered by the use of alcohol. Roseman had not studied chemistry since high school and had only the sketchiest understanding of what Decker was trying to get at with his proposed laboratory tests, but he was inclined to believe that the scientist knew what he was talking about. Roseman also appreciated that the experience and credentials of Decker's friend Altschule could be valuable not only in the laboratory but also in the courtroom: he could serve as an expert witness on Charles's mental condition.

After a seven-year association, Roseman and Decker now have good rapport, but their differing recollections of their first encounter suggest larger tensions about their respective roles in Charles's defense. Decker's overriding concern was to get his son tested. The legal questions that occupied Roseman — particularly, the conduct of Charles's trial — were decidedly secondary. Had Decker merely paid a retainer fee and told Roseman to do whatever he thought best to defend his son, the lawyer would have been the undisputed captain of the legal ship. Yet in this instance, Decker was not only intent on producing the evidentiary ammunition, he was also urging a particular line of attack.

Roseman himself acknowledges that Charles Decker's trial would have been quite different had he been the son of a mailman—or, for that matter, a lawyer—instead of an endocrinologist. Even so, he insists that the peculiar circumstances of the assaults would immediately suggest the insanity defense to any experienced lawyer. While he might not have been able to deploy biochemical evidence without Decker and Altschule's participation, he is sure that he could have built a good case on conventional psychiatric testimony.

Nicholas Decker's active role in the case put Roseman in a somewhat awkward professional position. Technically, he was representing Charles and owed undivided loyalty to him. Several days after meeting the father, he traveled to the Massachusetts Correctional Institution at Bridgewater, met Charles, and got the young man's permission to act as his lawyer. Yet the senior Decker was paying all the bills. It was Nicholas Decker, not his son, who had conceived of the testing and was insisting on it. Roseman, though struck with Decker's scientific detachment ("It is pretty unusual to have a parent looking at his son and saying, in effect, Is this fellow sick or is he a criminal?"), was convinced that whatever the father's personal motives, the tests were also in the boy's best interest. Were it otherwise, he could not have sought them in Charles's name.

With a modest-paying job as landscaper and with a young family to support, Charles had no way of making the $50,000 bail that had been set. By contrast, his parents' old farmhouse constituted more than enough collateral to secure Charles's release; but Decker was not about to bail him out even as a means of getting him into a hospital for tests. According to Roseman, "He wasn't comfortable with having his son released until he knew what he had on his hands." Roseman discounts as purely academic any tension between his obligations toward the son and his ties with the father. "Charles had no resources at all. So if I got into a fight with the father about getting bail, it wouldn't have helped Charles. That would have been frivolous on my part."

*

Frank O'Boy, the prosecutor in *Commonwealth v. Decker*, anticipated the insanity defense long before the Deckers retained David Roseman. O'Boy was involved in the case within three weeks of Charles's arrest. The fact that Charles had been sent to Bridgewater right away suggested that insanity might be claimed, a suspicion confirmed by Nicholas Decker's hurried conversation with O'Boy after the probable-cause hearing. The main thing, according to O'Boy, was that "there really was no other avenue open to the defendant."

The insanity defense is almost always a plea of last resort. If a criminal defendant thinks he can raise a reasonable doubt about whether he actually committed a crime, there is little incentive for him to slander himself—and risk confinement in a mental institution—by impugning his own sanity. Thus, though madness may actually explain many lesser crimes, it is invoked disproportionately in murder cases. After all, an insanity defense is expensive to litigate. Much must be at stake to justify the burden of pretrial examinations, witness fees, and added legal charges. Moreover, winning such a case can prove a Pyrrhic victory. The hero of Ken Kesey's *One Flew Over the Cuckoo's Nest* feigned looniness to get transferred from a prison to an asylum, but to most people a short jail sentence probably looks somewhat better than an indeterminate term in a mental hospital. Even after release, the person must live with the double stain of criminality and insanity.

From the outset Frank O'Boy had no serious doubts about Charles Decker's sanity—and still does not. "I felt that Decker did it and that he was mentally responsible for what he did. And nothing Dave came up with either before or during the trial caused me to alter my feelings." In O'Boy's view, it was essentially an open and shut case, one that only by luck was not a double murder. He was convinced that the brutality of Charles's attack and the severity of the girls' injuries mandated strict punishment.

Nevertheless, O'Boy had professional sympathy with Roseman. He, too, had defended clients in criminal cases, during nine years of private practice. He understood Roseman's responsibilities and problems, just as Roseman, himself a former prosecutor, had a good sense of how O'Boy was likely to approach a case.

Although Roseman and O'Boy shared the experience of working both sides of the street, the contrasts between the two men are more striking than their similarities. Roseman went from private school in Connecticut to Tufts College, graduating in 1952, then on to Columbia Law School. O'Boy's education was decidedly parochial. From Monsignor Coyle High in Taunton, Massachusetts, he went twenty-five miles southwest to Providence College, then twenty-five miles in the other direction to Boston College Law School. Roseman settled into a small but established law firm in the city. O'Boy returned to Taunton, an old New England mill town that has survived economic decline, and went into practice with the mayor.

After nine years in private practice, O'Boy was offered a position as a prosecutor in an adjacent county. His first reaction was to laugh. The state then paid its assistant district attorneys so little — about $11,000 a year — that it had to allow them to handle private cases as well. Even so, the time he could devote to his hard-built practice would be halved, while most of his office expenses would continue. O'Boy describes the circumstances of his decision thus: "When Phil Rollins, who used to be the D.A. for Cape Cod and the islands, asked me in 1973 if I wanted to join his office, I said, 'Why would I?' Rollins said, 'It'll add a line to your obituary.' "

The pay was modest and the workload great, but O'Boy enjoyed a great deal of discretion over the way in which he handled his cases. It was for him to decide what charges to bring, and, if a defendant was willing to plead guilty to a less severe count, what terms would be acceptable. O'Boy was also free to decide how much effort a particular case deserved. For a typical noncapital case, O'Boy might spend five or six hours to prepare the prosecution. The novelty of the insanity defense argued by Roseman, and the unusual amount of pretrial maneuvering, ultimately meant that the prosecutor had to give the Decker case ten times his normal effort. Even so, that was a mere fraction of the more than five hundred hours Roseman and his law associates spent to construct the defense.

Litigating on a helter-skelter basis can be demanding, but it greatly broadened O'Boy's courtroom experience. While a prosecutor, Roseman had been involved in several cases where capacity to stand trial was in issue, but he had never actually tried an insanity case (a fact Decker may not have known when he retained him). By contrast, O'Boy, though ten years Roseman's junior, had handled a number of insanity cases both as a prosecutor and as a defense counsel. Nonetheless, Roseman did not think he was at a disadvantage: "If you are a trial lawyer, you know the important territory. You always have to educate yourself about the facts of a particular case, but what you learn handling a tort claim or a patent dispute can be very helpful in a criminal trial."

O'Boy's overall experience has convinced him that it is extremely difficult, though not impossible, to get a verdict of not guilty by reason of insanity. In his view, part of the difficulty is a question of evidence. "A lot of jurors — and judges, too — feel that psychiatry is a pseudoscience." In the Decker case, O'Boy realized that if Roseman were able to introduce some sort of precise laboratory findings to buttress or even replace conventional psychiatric testimony, the defense might be able to hurdle this obstacle. Even so, O'Boy felt that the defense would have a problem with Charles's apparent dangerousness. A defendant who is found not guilty by reason of insanity is not necessarily released (a point of law Roseman researched at some length). Under Massachusetts statute such a person may be committed involuntarily to a state hospital for reexamination, to see if his release would cause the "likelihood of serious harm." If so, the defendant, though acquitted of the crime, can be held until he is no longer regarded as dangerous—conceivably for life. By contrast, a defendant who is found to have been temporarily insane at the time of the crime can walk out of the courtroom a free man.

In theory, the option of involuntary commitment should allay the concerns of a jury or judge about acquitting a person they regard as still dangerous. The issue might seem simply to be whether the defendant should go to prison for a specific term or be confined to a hospital until cured. O'Boy does not believe that the theory is borne out in practice, however, at least in southeastern Massachusetts where he practices and where Decker was to be tried. "Bridgewater State Hospital isn't far and Taunton State is right here. People know that somebody who is committed may be walking the streets in a couple of months," he says. Charles, in particular, would present any court with a dilemma: if it concluded that he was crazy, it would send him to a hospital that had already declared him sane.

O'Boy's and Roseman's contrasting experience and professional environment certainly affected the way in which they approached the Decker case, but it was their differing roles as prosecutor and defense counsel that defined their functions and ethical responsibilities. Lawyers who do divorce and personal-injury work follow the same principles whether they represent the husband or the wife, the plaintiff-pedestrian or the defendant-driver. By contrast, O'Boy believes that a prosecutor in a criminal case is under much stricter ethical constraints than is a defense lawyer.

O'Boy believes that it is essential for the adversary system to allow the defense much freer rein. "I don't think a defense counsel should concern himself over whether his client is guilty or not. You have a vast establishment that's trying to prove this fellow guilty. The defense counsel's job is—within the canons of ethics and the bounds of the law—to see that his client gets a fair trial, whether he is guilty or not." Asked if he would have any misgivings as a defense lawyer about asserting an insanity defense even if he himself believed his client to be perfectly sane, O'Boy answers, "None whatsoever."

In the case of Charles Decker, O'Boy first had to satisfy

himself as to the defendant's mental health, before going ahead with the prosecution. Even though he was persuaded that Charles was sane, he had no quarrel with Roseman doing his utmost to prove otherwise. He thought, though, that Roseman had a tough case to argue.

*

Although O'Boy and Roseman had never met before the case, each credits the other with being fair throughout the proceedings. O'Boy appreciated being kept informed about Dr. Altschule's laboratory findings, and Roseman notes that the prosecutor was cooperative in responding to the defense's pretrial motions. On some matters there was no need to fight. When Roseman took on the case in early October, Charles still had not been indicted. As prosecutor, O'Boy understandably wanted to move the case forward, but Roseman needed a formal indictment as well, for without it Charles was in something of a legal limbo. In August the district court, which has jurisdiction over less-serious crimes, had found probable cause to refer the case to a grand jury, but nothing had happened since.

The grand-jury system has come under attack in recent years. The fact that defense lawyers are not permitted to participate usually means that a prosecutor can take a grand jury wherever he wants. Recalling his experience in the United States Attorney's Office, Roseman says, "You just never lose in the grand jury." In some instances, prosecutors use the session to put key witnesses on the stand to see how they will perform in court. O'Boy, however, had no such need, having already had Gail Sussman testify at the probable-cause hearing.

In the Decker case, indictment was just a formality, but it gave Roseman a new forum (the Superior Court) in which to move to have Charles tested. The motion presented both Roseman and O'Boy with difficult tactical choices. Fledgling lawyers are taught that when the facts are unfavorable they should argue the law; when the law is against them they should argue the facts. Roseman confronted a situation in which he could find no specific legal precedent, either for or against the testing. Following the adage, he argued the facts. In his four-page memorandum in support of the motion to transfer, the only case he cited merely defined the Massachusetts standard for insanity. Instead of citing precedent, he explained the purpose of the proposed tests in great detail. "Defendant would be attempting to show," he wrote, "that consumption of alcohol by Defendant causes a biochemical malfunction which produces violent behavior in the Defendant." If verified, Roseman maintained, this malfunction would constitute a mental disease or defect within the meaning of the criminal-insanity law. To add weight to his plea he drafted an affidavit for Dr. Mark Altschule that began with an impressive summary of Altschule's credentials: teaching positions at Harvard, Yale, and Boston University; specialization in the physiology and biochemistry of stress reactions; hundreds of articles and "six or eight" books. Altschule and Nicholas Decker accompanied Roseman to the late-November hearing, prepared to elaborate on their plans in the event that O'Boy challenged their motion.

Given Roseman's inability to cite authority for his motion, O'Boy had grounds to challenge it. From his point of view, the case would be far simpler if the testing were not done. O'Boy was already conversant with standard psychiatric explanations of insanity and could easily argue the case on those terms. Moreover, if testing was allowed, it seemed unlikely that there could be any plea bargaining, at least at this stage. The father's immediate concern seemed to be with diagnosing his son's problem, if indeed there was one, rather than with the ultimate disposition of the case. Even if O'Boy were willing to recommend a light sentence in return for a plea of guilty to assault and battery (and O'Boy was not inclined to be that lenient), it seemed unlikely that the senior Decker would wish to have Charles released without a more complete medical investigation.

Yet O'Boy assented to Roseman's motion, despite the fact that it clearly signaled more work for the prosecutor. He notes, "If I had thought the whole thing were a sham, I would have objected, but I didn't." In part O'Boy was practicing professional courtesy, following his principle that the defense should have every reasonable opportunity to prove its case. But he was also savvy enough to avoid a potential legal trap. If he succeeded in persuading the trial court to veto the experiments, he would hand Roseman a procedural issue to appeal in the event of a conviction. Giving rope to one's opponent can be both an act of generosity and a way of letting him hang himself.

*

Having received the prosecution's assent, Roseman's motion was allowed the day after it was filed. The legal problem that Nicholas Decker had come to believe was intractable was resolved almost as a matter of routine. Decker and Altschule were now apparently free to begin their tests. But while they were preoccupied with the medical aspects of the case, Roseman — and O'Boy — had to be concerned with its changing legal dimensions.

Before Roseman could try the case, he had to know if the kind of abnormality Dr. Altschule suspected in Charles would come within the legal definition of insanity. He also had to find out how to get Altschule's expert opinion admitted, for Altschule was not a psychiatrist, in spite of his impressive credentials. Each legal question Roseman investigated seemed to suggest at least one more. In each case he read, references to other cases formed links in a chain of research that seemingly had no end. Roseman had not studied criminal insanity since he was a law student more than twenty years earlier, and much had changed in that time. Young associates found some recent cases for him, but Roseman himself prowled through his firm's library tracking down cases, copying important decisions, and underlining key passages in bright red ink.

At first blush the Massachusetts rule on criminal insanity might not seem to require extensive study. The test, adopted by the state's highest court in a 1967 opinion, *Commonwealth v. McHoul,* was drawn from the American Law Institute's Model Penal Code. It provides that "a person is not responsible for criminal conduct if at the time of such conduct as a result of mental disease or defect he lacks substantial capacity either to appreciate the criminality (wrongfulness) of his conduct or to conform his conduct to the requirements of the law." Although the ALI provision is succinct, its every phrase embodies legal principles that have evolved over centuries. An understanding of the history of the insanity defense is prerequisite to applying it to contemporary cases.

The policy of special treatment for the insane is not new, nor are the problems of determining in particular cases who qualifies for exemption from criminal penalties. In 1641 the Massachusetts Bay Colony adopted a law which provided that "Children, Idiots, Distracted persons, and all that are strangers or new comers to our plantation, shall have such allowances and dispensations in any case as religion and reason require." It was not difficult to determine who was a child, or a stranger. For example, an Indian was whipped and exiled, but not executed, for raping a white woman. But the matter of determining whether a defendant was distracted required more care. The law itself provided no definition. In 1688, Mary Glover—the only person in colonial Massachusetts who willingly confessed to being a witch (she was said to have caused fits in children)—was examined for several hours by a half-dozen physicians. They ultimately found her rational, hence by their standards sane.

The most advanced medical theory then held that insanity was invariably due to physical ailment of the brain. Mental disease as a defect of the mind was becoming untenable because physicians and philosophers agreed that the mind and the soul were intertwined. The God-given soul must be pure, thus only physical illness or injury could explain insanity. This view dominated medical theory, and legal definitions of insanity, until close to the beginning of the twentieth century. While this conception narrowed the availability of the defense, it was nonetheless used successfully in some instances.

Like most statutes and cases on insanity that have followed, the policy of the colonists that idiots and distracted persons should have special dispensation and allowances carries an implication of being self-evident. Yet to say that the insane, like children, should not be held responsible for their criminal acts is not to say why. Indeed, though the colonists believed that dispensation was appropriate in most cases, they did not permit insanity to excuse defendants of capital crimes. Retribution apparently outweighed compassion. (Idiocy, by comparison, was a defense in all instances. In 1692, for example, an Andover, Massachusetts, woman was convicted of being a witch, but was let off because she was "simplish.") Some scholars have concluded that the insanity defense is merely the obverse of the prosecution's duty to prove *mens rea*, or criminal intent. One who cannot be found to have rationally intended the consequences of his act should not be held guilty. Others explain that if one of the prime functions of criminal law is to discourage antisocial behavior, it makes little sense to punish those who cannot comprehend the rules. "The principle of criminal irresponsibility," the Massachusetts court concluded in *McHoul*, "is to maintain the general and specific deterrent effect of criminal penalties for wrong conduct, subject only to recognition of the injustice of punishing those lacking the capacity to appreciate the wrongfulness of, or to control, their behavior."

Laws that neither define their standards nor fully state their purposes leave a great deal of latitude to the courts responsible for applying them. Hence the applicability of the insanity defense was long decided on a case-by-case basis. Over the years, instructions in well-known cases came to be regarded as the law on insanity. In *Rex v. Arnold,* an influential eighteenth-century English case, there was evidence that the defendant was suffering from delusions when he took a shot at one Lord Onslow. The trial judge, however, cautioned the jury, "It is not every kind of frantic humor or something unaccountable in a man's actions, that points him out to be such a madman as is to be exempted from punishment; it must be a man that is totally deprived of his understanding and memory, and doth not know what he is doing, no more than an infant, than a brute, or a wild beast."

Later courts largely ignored the full logic of the instruction and simply seized on the phrase "wild beast." If rigidly applied, the wild-beast test would cover only a small fraction of the defendants we regard as truly insane today. Someone suffering from paranoid delusions, no matter how extreme, would not come under it. Nor would Charles Decker. Though his attack on the two girls was brutal, he certainly appeared civilized both before and after.

The vagueness of the insanity rule led to inconsistency in its application, and certainly allowed juries to reach controversial verdicts. In 1843 Daniel M'Naghten was tried in England for the murder of the secretary of Prime Minister Robert Peel, whom he had mistaken for the statesman himself. M'Naghten (whose name is spelled at least four different ways in the law books) suffered from the delusion that he was being persecuted by Peel's Tory party. While M'Naghten appeared rational in many respects, a physician testifying in the case told the jury that "monomania" (paranoia, in twentieth-century terminology) may exist in one who is generally sane. The judge instructed the jury that if it determined that the prisoner had not been "sensible" at the time of the shooting—that is, if he did not know he was "violating the laws both of God and man"—then they must find in the defendant's favor.

M'Naghten was acquitted. There was such a public outcry that the House of Lords polled the highest criminal-court judges in England to determine for the first time a uniform definition of criminal insanity. The result was the famous M'Naghten rule. Though criticized almost from the start and now largely superseded by later formulas, the rule contained elements that still influence modern law. It provided that a person invoking the insanity defense must prove beyond a reasonable doubt that while committing the act he "was labouring under such a defect of reason, from disease of the mind, as not to know the nature and quality of his act; or, if he did know it, that he did not know what he was doing was wrong."

The M'Naghten rule is also known as the right-and-wrong test. Its key is the defendant's knowledge at the time of the crime. A person who is so disoriented that he does not know he is using a gun is excused, as is one who is so deranged as not to know that using a weapon can be wrong. Had Daniel M'Naghten been held to such a test, he would have been convicted. He knew precisely what he was doing when he fired the gun (even if he confused his target), and, while his delusion made him feel that murder was his only recourse, there was no evidence that he did not know it was unlawful.

Chief Justice Lemuel Shaw, a dominant figure in nineteenth-century jurisprudence (and the father-in-law of Herman Melville), adopted the M'Naghten rule and improved upon it. Shaw elaborated on the knowledge requirement, holding that the accused must rationally understand "the relation in which he stands to others, and in which others stand to him." Thus M'Naghten, who suffered from a delusion by which he misperceived his relationship with Peel, might be spared under Shaw's broader Massachusetts rule.

Even with this modification, the M'Naghten rule was vulnerable to criticism from the medical profession that the emphasis on cognitive functions — knowledge of the act and of right and wrong — unduly overshadowed volitional processes. Apparently recognizing this, Shaw grafted another branch onto the test. Once it is established that the mind of the accused is diseased and unsound, he wrote, the question becomes "whether the disease existed to so high a degree, that for the time being it overwhelmed the reason, conscience and judgment, and whether the prisoner...acted from an irresistible and uncontrollable impulse."

Shaw's "irresistible impulse" test allowed judges and juries to consider emotional aspects of a defendant's behavior. The defense was of no use, however, to someone who planned his crime, as premeditation is inconsistent with the notion of a sudden impulse. Charles Guiteau, as crazy as he seemed, was hanged for the assassination of President Garfield because he could not find shelter under either the irresistible-impulse test (he spent days plotting his attack) or the M'Naghten rule (he was lucid, for the most part, and had practiced a little law, so he surely knew that murder was illegal).

Irresistible impulse is probably the most familiar of the legal tests for insanity, yet it, too, has been criticized on both medical and legal grounds, for it does not clearly distinguish between insane acts and merely criminal ones. Who after all is to say that an impulse is truly irresistible? That a defendant surrendered to an impulse does not necessarily mean that he had to. Strict believers in psychogenic theory reject the metaphor of the impulse with its suggestion of a highly charged bolt overpowering the normal, responsible circuitry of the brain. The mind is integral, they contend, and it is misleading to depict emotional processes as involving struggles between distinct forces of good and evil. (Neurologists and others, such as Mark Altschule, who look for physical stimuli of behavior might not be as quick to reject the image, and the law it reflects.)

As psychiatric theory grew more sophisticated after the turn of the century, the medical profession became increasingly vocal in attacking both the M'Naghten rule and the irresistible-impulse test as being artificially narrow. Behavior, the critics stressed, is a function of the entire personality.

Dramatic change in criminal-insanity law, however, did not come until 1954 and Judge David Bazelon's famous opinion *Durham v. United States.* A District of Columbia court had convicted Monte Durham of housebreaking, notwithstanding psychiatric testimony that had linked his crime to a long history of delusions and strange behavior. The trial judge had ruled that the evidence failed to establish either that the defendant did not know the difference between right and wrong or that he was in the grip of an irresistible impulse. Writing for the Federal Court of Appeals, Bazelon reversed the conviction and overturned the traditional law on which it was based.

Bazelon called the M'Naghten rule a "strait jacket," contending that "it does not take sufficient account of psychic realities and scientific knowledge." His fundamental objection to the test was not simply that criminal responsibility was made to rest on an invalid or indeterminable symptom, but that it had to rest on any particular symptom. "In attempting to define insanity in terms of a symptom, the courts have assumed an impossible role, not merely one for which they have no special competence," he wrote. Bazelon was equally hard on the irresistible-impulse approach, declaring that "it gives no recognition to mental illness characterized by brooding or reflection." In place of these traditional standards, Judge Bazelon established a new test under which defendants would be found not guilty if their criminal acts were "the product of mental disease or defect."

In many quarters the *Durham* decision was celebrated as signaling that criminal law, by allowing free admission of psychiatric testimony, at last was moving from the nineteenth century into the twentieth. Some state and federal courts endorsed the "product rule," as Bazelon's test came to be known, and even in jurisdictions that did not, *Durham* may have encouraged some relaxation of evidentiary limitations. In the trial courts of the District of Columbia, the practical impact of the rule was pronounced. Before *Durham* fewer than one percent of all criminal defendants had been found not guilty by reason of insanity. Under the new rule, that statistic jumped to five percent.

There were, however, two aspects of the *Durham* rule that ultimately led to its undoing. One was the seemingly straight-forward concept of "mental disease or defect." As should have been apparent from the outset, the medical profession's view of what constitutes a mental disease is subject to rapid change. That fact was driven home in 1959 when the participants at a psychiatric conference voted to classify sociopathy as a disease for the first time. In effect, doctors — not judges — were amend-ing criminal law by providing a defense to a class of people who had had none before. Concern also grew that juries were too deferential to experts. It had been expected that specialists would address only the question of mental disease, but as a matter of practice their testimony could not avoid touching on the issue of causation, which was supposed to be the province of the jury. In 1972, in *United States v. Brawner,* Bazelon's court scrapped the *Durham* rule in favor of the American Law Institute's new standard, largely on the ground that the "prod-uct" formula had proved unworkable. Bazelon himself joined in the decision, but his long concurring opinion warned that the ALI approach would not necessarily solve the problems that had been found in the *Durham* rule.

*

The ALI standard adopted in *Brawner* was the same test the Massachusetts Supreme Judicial Court had ratified five years earlier in *Commonwealth v. McHoul*. It was this rule that David Roseman and Frank O'Boy had to parse in planning their strategies for Charles Decker's trial. Though some parts of the ALI rule are new—it speaks not of "insanity" but "responsibility," to underscore that the ultimate judgment is social, not medical—it is in many respects a hybrid of earlier laws.

Like its predecessors, the ALI/*McHoul* rule tests responsibility "at the time of" the criminal conduct. For Roseman this meant that conceivably Charles could still be excused from punishment even if the court accepted the findings of the Bridgewater State Hospital report that he was not mentally ill during the twenty-day observation period. It was not clear at the outset whether Altschule would find that Charles suffered from a permanent abnormality, or that his condition had merely been transient. In theory, either would satisfy the legal test, but temporary insanity is usually a harder case to make, if only because it is difficult after the fact to prove the existence of an ephemera. Moreover, because an acquittal on temporary insanity absolves a defendant from incarceration in either a prison or an asylum, courts may be reluctant to find in favor of anyone who seems even remotely dangerous.

Just like the *Durham* rule it replaced, the ALI standard requires a causal connection between a defendant's mental impairment and his unlawful act. Where *Durham* required a showing that the act was the "product" of illness, the ALI provision speaks of disease resulting in incapacity either to appreciate the criminality of one's conduct or to conform that conduct to the requirements of law. The change in the language was intended to emphasize to courts and juries that the question of causation does not necessarily require medical expertise.

The most important connection between *Durham* and the ALI rule is use of the phrase "mental disease or defect." Endorsing that rule in *McHoul*, the Massachusetts Supreme Judicial Court declared that the "single greatest point" for it is that "experts will be unrestricted in stating all that is relevant to the defendant's mental illness."

Roseman underlined this passage, highlighted it, and wrote "key" in block letters in the margin. The opinion stood for the principle of full inquiry, and spoke of experts, not just psychiatrists. He could use the case first to justify Dr. Altschule's appearance as a witness, even though he was not a psychiatrist, and then to support the admissibility of the results of the laboratory tests Altschule was planning. Indeed, Roseman was encouraged by a further observation of the court: "A defendant's sanity comes to trial in cases where psychiatrists can and do hold and state opposing views. All such cases show that psychiatry is far from an exact science and that whether a defendant is to be called sane or insane cannot depend on any certain measurement." The lawyer read the statement as hinting that the court might attach greater status to his laboratory evidence than to conventional psychiatric testimony. "Laboratory tests are essentially objective and involuntary," says Roseman. "Charles had no control over what his blood counts would be or what chemistry was found in his body."

If Altschule was able to document an abnormality, the ALI/*McHoul* rule would further require proof that it caused "substantial incapacity" (Roseman noted that the incapacity did not have to be complete) in one of two respects. A defendant could show that he lacked the capacity to "appreciate the criminality (wrongfulness) of his conduct," or he could show an inability to conform his conduct to the requirements of law. The first provision, of course, is a descendant of the M'Naghten test of knowing right from wrong, and the difference between the two standards is essentially one of degree. "Appreciate" is intended to require more than a superficial knowledge. Under M'Naghten, a defendant who is capable of saying, "Yes, I know that murder is illegal," is deprived of the defense. Appreciation under the ALI test means a deeper assimilation of such knowledge.

While it was possible that Dr. Altschule would find a condition that rendered Charles Decker incapable, if only temporarily, of this degree of appreciation, the circumstances of the attack made it seem more likely that he would come under the second aspect of incapacity, that is, an inability to conform one's conduct to the requirements of law. Roseman was prepared to argue that even if Charles knew that what he was doing was wrong, he suffered from a mental impairment that left him unable to control himself. This, of course, was the old irresistible-impulse approach in a new form. While the change in language did broaden the defense by making it available to those whose behavior is triggered by long-standing psychoses, it still did not resolve the problem of causation, an issue no less profound than that of free will versus determinism. Medical experts could debate whether or not a mental disease or defect had deprived Charles Decker of his self-control, but a court would have to make the ultimate diagnosis.

*

For David Roseman and Frank O'Boy, the ALI/*McHoul* standards defined the terms on which Charles Decker would be tried, but both lawyers had to go further with their legal research. Roseman had to study all the insanity cases after *McHoul* to see how the standards had been applied in different circumstances. (O'Boy already was familiar with the principal decisions.) Both lawyers needed to have legal precedent at hand for pretrial motions and evidentiary questions. Roseman was concerned not only with the trial but with building a good record in case his client was convicted and it was necessary to appeal. The newer decisions not only elaborated on the *McHoul* principles but also, by revealing the tactics and arguments of other lawyers, gave Roseman and O'Boy clues on how to handle the Decker case.

The lawyers were in a somewhat anomalous position. Ordinarily it is the prosecutor who thrusts and the defense counsel who must parry, but in this instance Gail Sussman's testimony at the probable-cause hearing clearly had established a prima facie case of attempted murder. The burden was on Roseman to develop the insanity defense to rebut it. Moreover, while it is a prosecutor's duty to move a case forward to satisfy a defendant's constitutional right to a speedy trial, Roseman regularly sought postponements of the trial so that further tests could be performed on Charles. And until Roseman's insanity evidence was apparent, O'Boy could not prepare a specific response to it.

In essence, Roseman had to argue that his client lacked the capacity to control himself during the attacks, if not before and after. Temporary insanity is a hard argument for a defense lawyer to make, but it also is a hard argument for a prosecutor to counter, for the only witnesses are the victims and the defendant himself. The best O'Boy could do was to gather evidence that would underscore the fact that Charles appeared rational and in control of himself immediately before and immediately after the attacks.

*

Roseman had the initiative in terms of when the case would be tried and what issues would be contested, but he was frustrated by the results of much of his legal research. Either he found little concrete authority for the positions he was set to take, or worse, the precedents he did find seemed to go against him. This absence of authority reflected the fact that most insanity cases are tried on conventional grounds and do not involve the use of physical evidence. Yet Roseman had no way of knowing whether lawyers in other states had used physical evidence to win acquittal at the trial level, and hence had left no reported record for him to invoke.

Roseman could not even be absolutely certain that he would be able to find a published court opinion dealing with a case like his if there was one. A lawyer looking for a case on point first has to scan general sources — treatises, law-review articles, statutory annotations — to find some sort of reference to specific cases. A judicial opinion usually refers to earlier precedents as authority, and there is an index, *Shepard's,* which is continually updated to record every instance in which a judicial decision is cited in later cases. Little glyphs in *Shepard's* signal whether the decision has been followed, overturned, or distinguished. In this way a lawyer can work forward and back in time.

The success of this method, however, rests largely on finding one parallel case on which the research can be built. At one point Roseman thought he had found such a decision. A footnote in a treatise on psychiatry and criminal law referred to a Wisconsin Supreme Court case that ostensibly stood for the proposition that physical evidence of brain abnormalities must be admitted in insanity trials; but the lead proved false.

There was, in fact, more recent and potentially more helpful precedent on the proof of organic brain defects. *United States v. Brawner,* for example, though usually cited for overturning *Durham* and establishing the ALI test in the Federal Court of Appeals for the District of Columbia, also involved the same evidentiary issues that confronted Roseman. Indeed, the facts in *Brawner* were quite similar to those with which Roseman had to work.

The defendant, Archie Brawner, had had his jaw broken in a fight at a party. He left in a rage (one of the witnesses said that "he looked like he was out of his mind"), got a gun, returned, and fired through a closed door, killing a man. The policeman who arrested him soon thereafter testified that Brawner appeared normal, spoke clearly, and did not seem to be drunk. Both the defense and the prosecution called experts, all of whom testified that Brawner was suffering from an abnormality that was of a psychiatric or neurological nature. One labeled it as an "epileptic personality disorder," while others used terms like "psychologic brain syndrome associated with a convulsive disorder," "personality disorder associated with epilepsy," and "explosive personality."

There were two specific issues in *Brawner* that had a possible bearing on Charles Decker's situation. First, the prosecutor and, to some extent, the trial judge seemed concerned about whether a physical abnormality may constitute a mental disease or defect within the meaning of the insanity defense. The appellate court indicated that it clearly could. More important, the court criticized the prosecutor for trying to ridicule evidence of the defendant's brain defects. The organic damage had been diagnosed through a history of epileptic seizures, an abnormal electroencephalogram test, and the results of psychological tests, using drawing exercises and Rorschach projections as well as psychiatric interviews and observations. The prosecutor had zeroed in on the psychological tests, mocking the defense's case as resting on "just blots of ink." The court of appeals stated, "The prosecutor, who speaks in court in behalf of the public interest, has responsibility to refrain from know-nothing appeals to ignorance." *Brawner* was rich with analysis of the problems involved in proving organic brain damage and included references to other authority, but because the legal indexes cite it for other issues, the defense in *Commonwealth v. Decker* apparently never found the case.

Roseman was confronted with other legal issues that needed investigation. One problem was that Dr. Altschule suspected that Charles's metabolic problems were associated with the consumption of alcohol, and, under Massachusetts law, voluntary drinking cannot be used to excuse crime. Even if someone has drunk himself into a blind stupor and has no idea what he is doing or has lost all self-control, he still will be held criminally liable. Though such a person may not have directly intended to do harm or break the law, he is held responsible for the consequences that flow from getting drunk. Were the law otherwise, a criminal could escape punishment by making sure he had alcohol on his breath if and when he was apprehended.

The Massachusetts law on drinking and crime threatened utterly to destroy Charles's defense. If the standard rule was applied to him, and if Altschule confirmed that his behavior was related to alcohol consumption, then the medical findings instead of exculpating Charles would incriminate him. It was crucial for Roseman to find some grounds for the court to treat his client as an exception to the general rule. Moreover, this presented a problem not just at the trial — where O'Boy would surely argue that since no one forced Charles to drink, he must accept the consequences — but also at the outset, when Roseman was seeking court permission to have Charles tested. The lawyer could not very well argue for the right to have the tests performed if the tests could not be expected to help the defense.

Roseman knew that it would be futile to argue for a reversal or even a modification of the established alcohol rule. Instead he argued that it never was intended to apply to situations like Charles's. The cases spoke of the voluntary consumption of alcohol. Those who are drugged unwittingly or against their will can use the resulting incapacity as a criminal defense. In Roseman's view, Charles's drinking was voluntary only in the sense that no one had forced beer down his throat. But if Charles did not know about his apparent metabolic problem, Roseman reasoned, he had not freely taken responsibility for the unforeseen outburst that was triggered.

Since during pretrial O'Boy had assented to the motion to have Charles examined, the issue of drunkenness—and Roseman's volition argument—had not really been tested. But success at this stage was no guarantee for Roseman that he would prevail at the trial. O'Boy was sure to argue strenuously that if Charles's condition were related to alcohol use, then by law it could not constitute a defense to the charges. Moreover, Roseman knew that his argument on volition could potentially turn on him. "If Charles knew that he had an underlying metabolic defect," he concedes, "if he knew that by drinking liquor he would precipitate toxic material which would go to his brain and which could someday cause him to go berserk, then one could say that his drinking alcohol was voluntary." Even if Charles did not know of the precise mechanism but was aware that alcohol for him sometimes did trigger rage, then he would have assumed the risk. If Charles had any history of drinking and violence, Roseman would have to work to keep it out of court.

*

Roseman had done a thorough search of all the Massachusetts statutes and cases that had any connection with the insanity defense, and he now felt conversant with its various nuances. Yet he was frustrated that he had found little concrete legal authority that would be useful to his client. Indeed, a number of the appellate-court decisions that Roseman read upheld convictions in the face of what seemed like compelling evidence of insanity.

On first reading, *Commonwealth v. Ricard* seemed a particularly disheartening precedent. The facts in *Ricard* were parallel to those in Charles's case in several important respects. At the trial there was uncontradicted testimony that Ricard was insane. Yet the jury had convicted him and, in a 1969 decision, Massachusetts's highest court had affirmed the guilty verdict. On one level *Ricard* was a stern warning to Roseman of the difficulty of proving insanity, even when solid evidence was available. But on another level Roseman found he could use the decision as a textbook on how he should present his case to the trial court, or, if need be, on appeal.

Delpha Ricard had shot and killed a man in New Bedford with whom he had had a fight earlier in the day. He sped away in his car, but turned himself in to the police the next morning, saying that he had heard on the radio that he had killed someone the night before. He was in tears and told police that he did not want to disgrace his family. New Bedford, of course, is only twenty miles from Rehoboth, where Charles attacked the girls. "It is an area," says Roseman, "that is not unused to violence."

Ricard was sent to Bridgewater State Hospital for observation, just as Charles was later, but in this instance, the examiners found their inmate to be incompetent to stand trial. Dr. Lawrence Barrows, then the assistant medical director at the institution, found that Ricard was psychotic for most of the year following the killing. The man had a history of alcoholism and delirium tremens and had been admitted to another state hospital just two years earlier. When Roseman read the court's opinion, he underlined in red the following description of Dr. Barrows's conclusion: "He found a 'chronic brain syndrome' (permanent damage) due to prolonged use of alcohol, paranoid delusions and lack of insight into reality."

Notwithstanding Barrows's uncontradicted testimony, the jury rejected Ricard's insanity plea and found him guilty of murder. His lawyer appealed, contending that the uncontroverted medical testimony compelled a finding that Ricard was not guilty by reason of insanity. The Massachusetts Supreme

Judicial Court dismissed the appeal and affirmed the conviction, ruling that although the evidence would have supported an acquittal, it did not require one.

Roseman regarded *Ricard* as "the closest case that I could find factually to our situation." As with his own client, there was an indication in *Ricard* that the defendant suffered from a brain problem. Ricard, like Charles, had turned himself in to the police full of remorse. That Ricard could be convicted in the teeth of uncontradicted medical testimony that he was insane was sobering indeed. The state's highest court had also flatly declared that defendants have no right to sound out jurors on their attitudes toward psychiatrists and insanity, and this seemed to make Charles Decker's case all the more difficult.

Roseman also saw hopeful signs in the *Ricard* opinion, however. The decision, he recalls, was "sort of a road map to get me started to design my case." He saw that it was essential to distinguish Charles's situation from the circumstances in *Ricard*. On this score the Supreme Judicial Court had given him an opening. The presumption that Ricard was sane had been buttressed by the fact that he might have been provoked by his fight with the victim. Yet the court had added that such a presumption would not be warranted "where it is plainly apparent from the evidence that the act committed is not one that a sane person would have committed," specifically, where the act could not be explained by "anger, revenge, rejection, jealousy, hatred, insult, intoxication, or the like."

Roseman seized on this point. He would have to emphasize that there had been no provocation that could account for Charles's behavior, and that by elimination of all other causes, the only explanation had to be a mental disease or defect. Ironically, the greatest threat to this strategy lay not with the prosecution's witness but with his own client. At the probable-cause hearing Gail Sussman had already testified that although the defendant had had several beers, he was not drunk. More important, she had said that his attack with the hammer had come out of the blue, that there had been absolutely no provocation on her part. Her statement had been transcribed and could be used to impeach her testimony if she changed her story at the trial.

The story that Charles told his father the night of the incident—and that Nicholas Decker repeated to Roseman at their first meeting—was somewhat different. He said that the girls had been teasing him in some way, that there had been sexual overtones. If in *Ricard* the earlier fight was sufficient to constitute possible provocation, then Charles's version could support the conclusion that he responded out of anger, rejection, or insult, to use the court's terms.

Who was telling the truth? It was possible that Charles was fabricating a feeble excuse for his behavior, but it was also possible that the girls were concealing the fact that they had goaded him. Roseman thought that even if Charles's account were the accurate one, his reaction was so out of proportion to any teasing that it still should be regarded as insane. Roseman also knew from *Ricard,* however, that a court might well not see it that way.

Under the Fifth Amendment a criminal defendant need not testify at his own trial, and no inference is supposed to be drawn if he does not. As a matter of practice, those who assert the claim of self-defense almost always take the stand to give their side of the story. By contrast, those invoking the insanity defense rarely do. A defendant who appears rational and in control of himself undercuts his own argument, and one who appears deranged may frighten or alienate the jury. The possibility that Charles would be interrogated about provocation only clinched Roseman's decision not to have his client testify.

Keeping Charles off the stand did not guarantee, however, that his story would not come out in court. While under observation at Bridgewater, he had discussed the incident in detail, and O'Boy had access to the records. If anything, Charles's hospital statement could be even more incriminating, for it suggested somewhat greater provocation. According to O'Boy, "In the hospital record, he had made a statement that they were teasing him, threatening to tell his wife, and that one of them grabbed the hammer and hit him with it first." If this came out, Roseman was prepared to argue that Charles's savage reaction still was out of line with any provocation. He had not, after all, been injured in the slightest. Still a judge or jury, skeptical or confused about Altschule's medical theories, might well conclude that the girls' actions explained the defendant's and might not ask why his reaction was so explosive.

The law favored Frank O'Boy in many respects, but his advantage was not complete. Recent state and federal court decisions had given contradictory signals as to whether a prosecutor could simply rest on the traditional presumption that all men are sane until proved otherwise, or whether he had an affirmative duty to produce concrete evidence of a defendant's sanity. Resolution of this issue can affect the shape and conduct of a trial: which witnesses are called and what evidence is submitted. Even more important, the burden of proof can determine who wins and who loses when all the evidence is finally weighed by the judge or jury. This is particularly true when the question is as subjective as that of a defendant's sanity. A defendant who could not establish his insanity by a preponderance of the evidence might still be acquitted if, instead, the burden was on the prosecutor to prove beyond reasonable doubt that the defendant was sane. State and federal law on this point was in flux; even while the Decker case was pending, important decisions were announced. In planning their arguments and tactics, O'Boy and Roseman were aiming at a moving target. The trend appeared to favor Roseman.

At the same time, Roseman faced a difficult dilemma in deciding how to contend with Gail Sussman's testimony. On the one hand, her story was the heart of the prosecution's case. At the trial O'Boy had her describe in bloody detail Charles's relentless attacks, first with the hammer, then later with the rock. But on the other hand, Dr. Altschule used her description of the events to diagnose Charles's brain problem. As a layman, Roseman saw the circumstances as sufficiently bizarre that they could only be explained by insanity. He hoped that a court would agree. He had come across judicial opinions stating that a crime may be so "dreadful" that the act itself constitutes evidence of insanity.

In some situations lawyers can plead in the alternative — that is, advance more than one argument for their cause — but in criminal cases such pleas may undercut one another. For example, a defendant cannot very easily claim that he was miles from the scene of the crime and at the same time invoke self-defense. Roseman could try to shake Sussman's story, but that might backfire. If on cross-examination he succeeded in getting her to admit that she had been teasing Charles, perhaps even to say that she had struck him first, such an admission could conceivably mitigate Charles's crime, but by establishing provocation it could at the same time devastate the insanity argument. By contrast, if Roseman simply let Sussman's story stand unchallenged, everything would ride on the insanity plea. "In a way," says Roseman, "it's a terrible trap for a defense lawyer. You want to say, boy, aren't these peculiar, violent facts. A rational mind wouldn't do this. There's something wrong. But the more you talk about the horrible nature of the alleged events, the more you're putting your fellow away."

To this day Roseman refers to Charles's attack on the girls as "alleged." "We never conceded that he did anything and I'm not about to concede anything now, or will I ever concede that he did." Given the young man's potential civil liability to the victims — and a lawyer's natural loyalty to his client — it is not surprising that Roseman emphasizes this position. Yet in his brief cross-examination of Sussman, he clearly was trying to reinforce her story, not challenge it. Rather than attacking the prosecution's witness, Roseman tried to reassure her.

"I just have a few questions, Miss Sussman. Now, up until the time Mr. Decker struck you with the hammer as far as you were concerned, he was acting normally. Is that correct?"

"Yes," Sussman answered simply.

"He didn't appear drunk to you?"

"No."

Roseman had Sussman confirm that they had been stopped by a policeman and that Charles was driving the car normally. He reminded her of the point at which Charles had left the car to go to relieve himself. "Then he came back and he sat in the car, and he started to rub his pants?" Roseman asked.

"Yes, that's so," said Sussman.

"Then you said he started to strike you with the hammer. Is that right?"

"That's right."

Through his leading questions, Roseman had quickly gotten to the point he wanted to make. "And, as a matter of fact, when he started to strike you with the hammer he had a real scary look on his face, did he not?"

"That's right," said Sussman. "He did."

Earlier, during O'Boy's examination, she had said of the defendant: "He seemed real mad. I don't know, really strange." Roseman wanted more, but perhaps overplayed his hand by saying, "He almost looked like a madman, did he not?"

"No," said Sussman, not about to bite. "He just looked really mean."

"And scary?"

"Yes," the witness conceded.

Roseman asked her to describe Charles's reaction after the second attack, when she tried to talk with him. "And when you started to calm him down he lost the scary look in his face?"

"No, he wasn't scary then."

"When you were calming him down he wasn't scary looking?"

"No," said Sussman, "he was frightened."

"What?" interrupted Judge Dwyer.

Sussman answered again: "Frightened or scared."

"Did he look sorry?" asked Roseman.

O'Boy started to object, but Sussman said, "Yes."

"I pray Your Honor's judgment," said O'Boy. The judge excluded the question as calling for too much of a subjective characterization, but Roseman had already gotten the answer he wanted, even if not for the record. Roseman went on to get the witness to describe how his client had tried to help the injured girls back in the car, how he had said that he was going to get them help, and how he got them to Santos' store safely.

"Did he attempt to help you out of the car?" asked Roseman.

"He went around, stopped the car, and he went around to the

passenger's side. And he opened the door, and he went to help me out, but I know I didn't want him touching me. He did enough. I didn't want him hurting or touching me any more."

"He attempted to help you?" persisted Roseman.

"Yes."

"Did he attempt to help Debbie?"

"No, because I had my arm around Deb to help her out myself."

"And that's the last you saw of him that night, that is, at the Santos' store. Is that right?"

"That's right," said Sussman.

Roseman walked back to the defense counsel's table and said, "No further questions."

\*

Roseman was not dissatisfied. If Sussman had balked at calling Charles Decker a madman, she had nonetheless reiterated for the court that he had been rational just before and just after the attacks, that the assault had come out of the blue, and that he had tried to get help for the girls afterward. Roseman certainly could not rely on Sussman's testimony to prove that his client was insane, but at least she had established a foundation on which Mark Altschule could construct his explanation of Charles's behavior.

Though not complacent, Roseman felt reasonably confident about his legal position. There were weaknesses in the case—most conspicuous the problems of voluntary consumption of alcohol and the admissibility of the damaging hospital records, with their disclosure of prior violence—but Roseman was heartened by the recent cases that seemed to place a heavier burden on the prosecution to rebut strong evidence of insanity. If Altschule could persuade the court that Charles in fact did suffer from some sort of brain abnormality, Roseman thought they had a good chance to prevail.

Lawyers, of course, have to guard against being beguiled by their own arguments. Charles Rembar, a noted civil-liberties advocate, has described the "singing-in-the-shower" syndrome, in which the lawyer preparing a case gets carried away with the tone and rhythm of his own song. Roseman uses a different metaphor, perhaps the result of his association with Altschule and Decker. "I look at a trial, if it's conducted properly, as sort of a laboratory. All of the fallacies, all of the self-serving positions, somehow get stripped away in this very civilized but brutalizing process we call the adversary system. It's all well and good if you're in your office and construct some theoretical, pie-in-the-sky defense, but you've got to ask yourself as everyone is puffing it up, how is it really going to play when it's being hammered at?"

# 4. Medicine

"I DON'T THINK there's another physician in the country who could have done what Mark Altschule did," insists Nicholas Decker.

Altschule has many such admirers scattered throughout the American medical profession and beyond: former students at various universities, colleagues who served with or under him on hospital staffs, and associates in a broad range of professional and interdisciplinary activities. To them, Altschule is original, broad-minded, brilliant, a profound philosopher and historian of medicine, and (in Decker's words) "one of the most amazing physicians who's been around in quite a long while — absolutely fantastic in his ability to make diagnoses."

Altschule's critics, and they too are legion, find the same man vain, cynical, opinionated, sometimes frivolous, often "impossible." This striking difference of opinion may be merely a matter of emphasis, however. Most of those on each side (and those who know Altschule generally take one side or the other) would grant the opposing claims. Altschule himself would probably admit the accuracy of both perceptions.

Mark Altschule is a short man with a large hearing aid. He is too solid to be called birdlike, but he has the bright eyes and alert gestures that term usually implies. Now in his mid-seventies, he looks his age, for his vigor and ebullience are not the properties of a younger man. They are qualities that, regardless of age, some have and most do not.

Today Altschule's headquarters — or one of them, for his is a very active retirement — is a corner office high in the Countway Library of the Harvard Medical School. Here he is close to both the school's alumni office, where he acts as a consultant, and Holmes Hall, the library's rare-book and manuscript collection, where he pursues his study of the history of medicine and psychology. In addition to producing the reams of articles that usually accompany a successful career in academic medicine, Altschule has written a half-dozen books on medical subjects and the same number on the history of medicine, and has further projects under way in both fields.

His accent is that of New York and City College, but the office is decidedly Harvard. The table at which he works once belonged to Oliver Wendell Holmes, Sr. He is at once an insider and an outsider, and as such can easily play the gadfly in his profession. Boston, of course, is a special place, medicine is a special field, and Boston medicine is a very special community indeed. Here, Altschule is — as both his admirers and his critics would agree — different.

A great part of Altschule's quirky nature is the provocativeness that marks the born teacher. Indeed, he regards himself as a teacher and physician by profession, and a scientist only incidentally. His professorship at Harvard was in the practice of bedside medicine, and he has spent a large part of his career as a champion of clinical medicine in a world of researchers. His bugaboos are the research-oriented physician who forgets that his first responsibility is always to the patient, and the medical scientist who does not understand that research must not only serve clinical practice but also must be inspired by it. "Research in medicine," he claims, "is not generally directed toward improving patient care — that is, it is, of course, but the number of people who do things that improve patient care is negligible. They don't do it for that reason."

His own research—for despite all his disclaimers, he had a laboratory for many years, and his name appears on hundreds of scientific articles—was undertaken in a different spirit. "I'm a doctor and I do clinical medicine," he says. "The reason I did research was that I'm a teacher. In order to explain things to the students, I had to explain things in terms of what they knew, even though it might be false. So when I studied the physiology and biochemistry of disease, they were always patient-related. I didn't care about this and that theory, because as soon as you get into that, you get further and further away from medicine."

Medical practice, too, is in essence a matter of explanation, according to Altschule. "In a sense, if a patient says to you, 'Doctor, I'm short of breath,' he's asking, 'Why am I short of breath?'" Teaching and practice, therefore, guide his research interests: "My interest in research, which is—fifty years, by God!—I started in 1929, published my first paper in '32, that's fifty years, isn't it—has always been directed at trying to have some kind of explanation consistent with the body of knowledge."

It is in this clinically based striving for explanation, rather than in artificial experiment in a cloistered laboratory, that Altschule finds the impetus for medical progress. "What happens is that the physician—and I say the *physician,* not the research man—finds that most of what he sees cannot be explained by current information." The clinician raises questions, and seeks answers, and thus creates science. "For example," Altschule points out, "all vitamins were discovered by doctors at the bedside, who saw something they couldn't understand, and wrote about it, and that created a lot of biochemistry. And every science—well, astronomy grew out of astrology, which the doctors were using as they use the electrocardiogram now, as sort of a chart. You can go down the list of all the sciences—anatomy to zoology, from A to Z—and they all, every one of them, grew out of what some doctor saw and could not explain." Altschule snorts at the alternative view: "The current idea that all this biochemistry and physiology is going to remake medicine is just nonsense, because medicine is remaking them, and it always will." But he acknowledges that the changes medicine induces in biochemistry sometimes reverberate to medicine.

Thus, when he insists that he is a clinician, Altschule is not deprecating his ability to make scientific contributions; on the contrary, in his view clinicians are the true scientific revolutionaries. One of his own earlier attempts to fulfill that role, however, was not successful. In the 1950s, he advanced the theory that a great deal of mental illness was due to dysfunction of the pineal gland. Several great figures in the history of science have lent their reputations to interpretations of the pineal gland's importance. At various times, it has been designated the controlling organ in growth, nutrition, sex, and race. To Descartes it was the pivot of the dualistic universe, the point at which the body and soul were joined. Mark Altschule, in turn, contended that one of the gland's true functions was to regulate the operation of the brain. He believed that many psychoses conventionally attributed to external emotional causes actually resulted from occasional failure of the pineal gland.

This theory, despite its author's persistent efforts to support it, was not well received in the medical world. Indeed, it was subjected to considerable ridicule. Altschule trimmed his sails, yet continued to monitor research on the pineal gland; as he pursued the Decker case, he was also at work editing a book on the subject. Indeed, investigating his patient's apparent limbic dysfunction seemed to promise a larger medical breakthrough.

"My interest in Charles Decker's case," he admits, "was twofold. I wanted to help the family, because they were my friends. I wanted to help them understand whether their boy was a monster, or whether he was a sick boy. If he were a monster, they were prepared to act. But if he were sick, they wanted something done about it. In addition to that, I had this vague and uneasy feeling that this was going to be a rather significant part of medicine in the future, after I'm dead. And I'd come back and laugh at them."

*

When Nicholas Decker turned to Altschule for help, he had good reason to believe that his old friend would be particularly interested in the questions raised by his son's case. Decker knew that one of the major aims of the physician's career was to reassert the claims and responsibilities of medicine in the treatment of mental illness, in the face of what he saw as the prevalence of abstract and often absurd psychoanalytic theory. For four decades he had fought to establish the proposition that much mental illness was caused not purely by psychic forces, but by physical dysfunction of the brain. During most of this period Altschule had been on the staff of McLean Hospital, the psychiatric unit of the Massachusetts General Hospital.

Located in Belmont, one of Boston's more pleasant suburbs, McLean's tree-shaded lawns and brick buildings look more like those of an exclusive preparatory school or small college than a mental hospital. Indeed, it long enjoyed a certain cachet as the refuge of overly eccentric Boston Brahmins and overwrought Harvard scholars. A proper Bostonian has been said to be someone with a pew in King's Chapel, a plot in Mt. Auburn Cemetery, and a relative in McLean. (The prevalence of medical insurance today has had the effect that the institution now serves a much more representative constituency.)

The hospital commemorates John McLean, who came down from Maine to Boston after the Revolution to make his fortune, and did. (Not without reverses; he was one of the first to make use of federal bankruptcy laws. A few years later, however, he was able to hold a dinner party for his former creditors, at which each found at his assigned place at table full repayment for his defaulted debts.) Although self-educated and without medical connections, McLean exemplified the public spirit his age valued so highly. When he died in 1817, he divided his estate between Harvard (to establish the first chair of modern history in America) and the Massachusetts General Hospital (for its most urgent project). Two years later the McLean Hospital opened its doors. Ever since, it has ranked among the most prestigious centers for care of the mentally ill, and for research into their afflictions.

From 1947 to 1968, Mark Altschule served McLean as director of internal medicine, with responsibility for the physical health of its patients and for research in clinical physiology. In the heyday of psychogenic psychiatry, in the midst of the enemy's camp, he worked almost single-handedly against that orthodoxy. When Nicholas Decker called Mark Altschule, he turned to a man who knew both sides of his issues, and who was also accustomed to controversy.

Altschule's first response to his friend's plea was to recall his own examination of Charles Decker some years before, following a less-serious outburst. On that occasion, he had suggested an endocrinological abnormality—an inappropriate secretion of insulin—in his patient, but had been unable to draw any further conclusions. Decker's secondhand report of this new assault revived his suspicion that some sort of brain dysfunction underlay Charles's violence. Seeking more details, he drove down to the district court in Taunton for the probable-cause hearing.

When Altschule heard Gail Sussman's account of the assault, he realized that he had misconceived his patient's problem. He had been thinking in terms of a chronic condition, a persistent mental ailment that occasionally revealed itself in aggression. Charles's actions, however, seemed clearly characteristic of a sudden seizure—a brainstorm that swept him from normality to assaultive violence, then plunged him into confusion and contrition.

To confirm his assessment, and to make it more precise, Altschule needed to move his patient to a setting where he could subject him to a series of endocrinological tests. McLean, where Altschule still was a consultant and knew the staff, was the obvious choice, and he found a psychiatrist there who was willing to collaborate. The district-court judge who first heard the case, however, summarily rejected the motion to move the prisoner. Charles sat in Bridgewater State Hospital (which did not have research facilities) for three months, until his father hired David Roseman to effect the transfer.

Decker and Altschule thought they had cleared the highest of their legal hurdles. Because Bridgewater is only fifteen miles from Rehoboth, the father chose to arrange the details of his son's transfer himself. When he kept his appointment with the director of Bridgewater State Hospital, however, Decker received a shock — "one of these criminal-justice-system events," he calls it today. As soon as he walked into the office, the director began listing the security precautions required for the transfer: two prison guards, off-duty but at full pay, to transport Charles, and one on duty around the clock throughout his stay at McLean, together with incidentals such as a mileage allowance. McLean's basic rate was then $125 a day, and Altschule's tests would be an additional, and substantial, expense. The guards would more than double a burden that Decker already could barely afford.

"It's impossible," he protested. "Look, I'm a scientist — I'm not one of these brain surgeons who can make that much money in one afternoon."

The director was taken aback. He told Decker that the transfer order, unprecedented in his experience and in the hospital's history, had led him to misunderstand the situation. "I thought you were one of those super society doctors who has more pull than the governor," he explained. "And that's what's been arranged. Now what the hell do you want to do?"

Decker explained the situation, and why he and Altschule wanted to transfer Charles. "If I come out at one end of this game," he concluded, "he'll be your tenant for life. Come out at the other, I want him walking the streets."

The hospital director was now more sympathetic. Moreover, he had a solution to the problem. He told Decker that the Commonwealth of Massachusetts maintained a secure hospital — the Lemuel Shattuck Hospital in Jamaica Plain — that cared for convicts whose medical problems were beyond the capabilities of prison infirmaries. Because prisoners were often used as voluntary experimental subjects, Shattuck also had adequate laboratory facilities and an expert staff with experience in research procedures. Best of all, the director pointed out, "If I send your son over there, it's done on the state's time, no charge;

the only thing you'll have to pay is your doctor, and I understand that he's doing it because he's a friend of yours and wants to get the answer. Can you afford that?"

"Yes," replied Decker, "that's just the size." This change of plans, however, meant more delay and more legal expense. The court order Roseman had obtained referred specifically to McLean Hospital and indicated that the defendant would assume all expenses. Given the seriousness of the criminal charges, the Bridgewater director could not take it upon himself to deviate from the court's instructions. Decker had to go back to Roseman and have him prepare a revised motion. But because the transfer had already been approved in principle—only the mechanics had to be worked out—there was no real concern about court permission this time. Roseman sent Mary Brody, a young associate, to present the motion. By the time the papers had been prepared, notice given, and the hearing held, it was mid-February, more than half a year after Charles Decker's alleged crime.

*

Franklin Park is the pendant of the "emerald necklace" laid out for Boston in the late nineteenth century by the great landscape architect Frederick Law Olmsted. Located among its vales, crags, and bowers, shaded pools and mellow stone bridges, the Lemuel Shattuck Hospital (named for the founder of the public-health movement in Massachusetts) is a raw brick-and-concrete high-rise. Outside its tall fence the pleasant curving drive is patrolled by police cars, which warn stopping automobiles to move along, and train a suspicious eye on loiterers on the public golf course across the way. If McLean looks deceptively like a prep school, Shattuck, like so many modern hospitals, resembles a mildly glorified prison. In this instance, that appearance is not misleading.

Upon admission to Shattuck, patients are routinely given a full examination by the hospital's medical staff, whose experience, because of the nature of their clientele, may be somewhat broader than that of their colleagues in more-ordinary institutions. In any case, Dr. William Timberlake, a well-known neurologist, observed something in Charles Decker that previous examiners had missed. He noted in his report, "question of Korsakoff's syndrome."

When Mark Altschule saw that notation he was surprised, and angry at himself. Korsakoff's syndrome (or the Wernicke-Korsakoff syndrome, as it is often termed) is, according to experts, regularly overlooked by internists who regard it as a rare curiosity. Altschule, however, had had extensive experience with the condition, and had published several articles about it. Although he had never actually given Charles a full examination, he felt that if the boy had it, he should have noticed it. He knew, moreover, that the condition is usually found among chronic alcoholics. Charles, despite his problems with drinking, certainly was not in that category. Timberlake, however, was sure of his diagnosis, and added that the resident in neurology had confirmed residual Korsakoff's. Altschule wanted to see for himself.

Korsakoff's syndrome (or Korsakov's or Korsakow's, depending on the system of transliteration from the Cyrillic alphabet) is a condition characterized by a failure of short-term memory, with a particular inability to recall verbal or semantic material. Sergei Sergeivitch Korsakoff himself described it, in 1889, as "an extraordinarily peculiar amnesia, in which the memory of recent events, those which just happened, is chiefly disturbed." At the same time, however, the subject generally retains his full intelligence and mental alertness, and attempts to conceal his amnesia from the interviewer by evasion or by fabrication of stories, plausible or implausible, to explain what he cannot remember. "At first," reported Korsakoff,

> during conversation with such a patient, it is difficult to notice the presence of psychic disorder; the patient gives the impression of a person in complete possession of his faculties; he reasons about everything perfectly well, draws correct conclusions from given premises, makes witty remarks, plays chess or a game of cards, in a word, comports himself as a mentally sound person. Only after a long conversation with the patient, one may note that at times he utterly

confuses events and that he remembers absolutely nothing of what goes on around him; he does not remember whether he had his dinner, whether he was out of bed. On occasion the patient forgets what happened to him just an instant ago: you came in, conversed with him, and stepped out for one minute; then you came in again and the patient has absolutely no recollection that you had already been with him.

Victims of Korsakoff's syndrome often attempt to distract attention from their problem by adopting an ingratiating manner. "To see a group of Korsakoffs in conversation at a mental hospital is charming," remarks Altschule. "They're always trying to please each other, but they don't know what the hell they're talking about. They remind me of the ordinary cocktail party." This tendency to cover up memory deficits and propitiate interlocutors by evasive or fabricated answers— confabulation—is the identifying factor used to diagnose Korsakoff's syndrome. As Altschule explains, "If you had Korsakoff's disease, I would say to you, 'Today's Friday. What day is it?' And you would say, 'Well, you just told me what day it is,' because you wouldn't know."

The standard test for the syndrome takes the form of a conversation between the examining physician and his patient. The examiner chats, apparently casually, throwing out bits of information as he goes. In reality he is carefully guiding the discussion through a series of circles, returning time after time to the same points to find out how much of the imparted information the subject retains in his memory, and for how long. The process is often lengthy and tedious, especially in mild cases. After almost two hours of talk with Charles Decker, however, Altschule knew Timberlake's diagnosis was correct.

Korsakoff's syndrome is today regarded as an extreme form of Wernicke's encephalopathy, a disease of the brain associated with a deficiency of thiamine (vitamin $B_1$). While many of those who suffer from the milder form can be treated with nutritional supplements, Korsakoff's itself is widely considered to be virtually untreatable, involving irreversible brain damage. It rarely kills its victims, but between one thousand and two thousand of them are admitted to American mental hospitals each year, and many never leave. The great majority of these are chronic alcoholics who tend to have poor, thiamine-deficient diets and whose condition inhibits the absorption of thiamine in the intestine. In 1978 the *New England Journal of Medicine* published a cost-benefit analysis of the syndrome's treatment, written by two California researchers who concluded that, at a much smaller price than the estimated $70 million annual cost of institutionalizing its victims, the Wernicke-Korsakoff syndrome could be virtually eliminated by the simple expedient of fortifying all alcoholic beverages with thiamine additives.

So although Charles Decker, a man in his early twenties, was not an alcoholic by any means, he was apparently suffering from an incurable condition associated with the advanced stages of long-term chronic alcoholism. Altschule knew that this was not unthinkable. Although several nineteenth-century researchers had identified the syndrome, it bears the name of Korsakoff, the great Russian psychiatrist, because he was the first to recognize that the condition could arise from causes other than alcohol.

Korsakoff's original article on the subject, which appeared in the Russian journal *Vestnik Psichiatrii* in 1887, was entitled "Disturbance of psychic function in alcoholic paralysis and its relation to the disturbance of the psychic sphere in multiple neuritis of nonalcoholic origin." He reported that almost a third of the cases he had encountered were unrelated to alcoholism. They had usually developed in the course of some other disease (such as typhoid, tuberculosis, or diabetes), to the bafflement of the attending physician. (This proportion of nonalcoholic cases is higher than that found in most studies — typically, more than ninety percent of Korsakoff's-syndrome patients in American mental hospitals are alcoholics — but it may be that the standards defining alcoholism were considerably stricter in Czarist Russia than they are in the United States today.) By contrast, an investigation of Wernicke's disease by two Scottish pathologists concluded that most cases of the milder condition were non-alcohol-related, but that these went disproportionately undiagnosed.

Korsakoff's realization that "cerebropathia psychica tox-aemia," as he called it, could occur without alcoholism enabled him to define its characteristics more precisely than his predecessors had, and indeed more accurately than those of his successors who still think of the syndrome as exclusively alcohol-related. He knew, for instance, that recovery from the condition was not unusual. (Altschule, like the Shattuck neurologists, found it in Charles only in residual form, and later all traces disappeared.)

Of paramount importance for Altschule, Korsakoff had connected irrational violent behavior with the classical amnestic confabulation that identifies the syndrome. The victim, Korsakoff wrote, may suffer "extraordinary agitation, anxiety, and indefinable fear. The patient cannot rid himself of obsessive anxious thoughts; he expects something terrible to happen...At times there are wild shouts, hysterical-like episodes..." He "upbraids the people around him, throws things at members of his household, beats his chest, and so on." In some cases, with or without anxiety, irritability, or the classical indications, the syndrome could appear "in the form of attacks of violence with confusion." This phrase, written by a Russian psychiatrist almost a century earlier, was a fair summary of the sudden onslaught Altschule had heard Gail Sussman describe at the probable-cause hearing.

Altschule was aware that legally the diagnosis of Korsakoff's syndrome cut both ways. On the one hand, it provided specific confirmation that Charles Decker was suffering from a neurological defect known to be related to violent behavior. On the other, the condition was, however inaccurately, often associated specifically with alcoholism, and under Massachusetts law the influence of alcohol is no defense to criminal charges. As David Roseman put it in a letter to the physician, "the voluntary use of alcohol or a drug which causes criminal irresponsibility makes unavailable to the user the defense of insanity because his mental condition was caused by his own hand." Altschule translates this to mean, "if you take a drink, and you do something to Aunt Mary, you are guilty because you chose to take the drink."

Altschule did not concern himself with the legal implications, however. ("I don't argue with legal theories, I assume they're wrong," he said.) From his point of view, the diagnosis of Korsakoff's syndrome was merely the icing on the cake; it merely added more information to support his contention that Charles had some kind of brain disease.

*

The clinical observations that guided Altschule's thought were not those of the long-dead Russian psychiatric reformer, nor even primarily those taken from his own examination of his now-quiescent patient. Instead, he relied on the observations of the two teen-age girls who had survived the assault—as interpreted through his own knowledge and experience. "What the girls described," he concluded, "was a seizure involving the temporal lobe, or rather the limbic system."

Human beings prefer to think of the brain as it appears from above: the great coiled and folded mass of the cerebral cortex, the seat of memory and imagination, divided (with implications we are only just beginning to understand) into two bulging hemispheres. The view from below is quite different, and reminds us that we are, after all, animals. The spinal cord, rising from the body, becomes the brainstem, or medulla, which controls instinctive behavior. To the rear, the cerebellum coordinates voluntary muscular functions. Above loom the various lobes of the brain, with their diverse roles in sensation, thought, and behavior. In the lower center, knitting the several parts into a single working organ, is the limbic system.

The limbic system is concerned with survival and emotion. Students of the brain like to say that its sphere of influence is "the four F's: feeding, fighting, fleeing, and sexual behavior." Another way of putting it is to say that the limbic system provides the connection between thinking and feeling. Humans have all the instinctive reactions of primitive creatures "wired in" to their brains, but they also have the ability to override their primitive instincts (seated in the brainstem) by applying their intelligence (seated in the cortex). In other words, they can stop and think. The limbic system, which links the lower and upper brains, makes this self-control possible.

The term *limbic system* was coined in 1952 by Dr. Paul MacLean of the National Institute of Mental Health, to replace the old name *rhinencephalon,* or "nose brain," which refers to the system's extensive links to the olfactory structures. The new neutral phrase, which alludes to the formation's position as a ring or cap around the brainstem, no longer hints at the important bit of evolutionary history suggested by the earlier term. When the first mammals appeared, the earth was ruled by dinosaurs. New creatures could not compete with these monsters by daylight; they were able to find an ecological niche in which they could survive only by adapting to life at night, when their warm blood gave them an advantage over reptiles made sluggish by cold. In making this adaptation, they became less dependent on vision, and evolved an immensely sophisticated sense of smell, which was more valuable for nocturnal foraging. Allowing for body size, the most primitive mammal has a brain four times bigger than any reptile's, and most of the increase is in the structures that process sensory data, facilitating interpretation rather than mere reaction.

In human beings, because of highly developed neocortical hemispheres, the limbic system represents only the inner fifth of the brain, so far have we come from the age of the reptiles. Without this legacy from our earliest mammalian ancestors, however, we could not have evolved at all.

Brain researchers have identified various components of the limbic system — the hypothalamus, mammillary body, septal area, amygdala, anterior thalamus, hippocampus, and so on — and, in many cases, determined which mental functions they control. Thus, for example, they have established that the hippocampus (the word means "seahorse," describing the organ's shape) plays a vital role in long-term memory formation, and that dysfunction in this region may be related to the most prominent symptom of Korsakoff's syndrome.

More important to Altschule, the limbic system, and specifically the small almond-shaped structure called the amygdala, plays a recognized role in violent behavior. When an electrical stimulus is applied to that area of an animal's brain, the creature stops in its tracks and displays signs of rage and fear. A dog growls, bares its teeth, and crouches to leap. In 1939 two researchers at the University of Chicago removed the amygdala of a monkey, and found that it became docile and lost its capacity for aggressive behavior, along with certain cognitive abilities. Other scientists have associated various types of epilepsy with abnormal electrical discharges in the limbic region.

*

Altschule, then, had several facts that seemed to fit loosely into a pattern. He knew that Charles Decker had a metabolic abnormality in which alcohol seemed to be implicated. He had found evidence of a physical dysfunction, known to be usually alcohol-induced, in the limbic area of the brain. Finally, he was aware that there existed a considerable amount of research establishing a connection between limbic disorders and violent assaultive behavior. He needed something to help him draw these thoughts together.

He found what he was looking for in a book called *Violence and the Brain*, published in 1970, by Vernon H. Mark and Frank R. Ervin, with an introduction by William W. Sweet. *Violence and the Brain* provided an organizing idea for Altschule's thinking, and ultimately for the entire case of Charles Decker in both its medical and legal aspects. David Roseman and Frank O'Boy each read the book with care. They still pepper their speech with terms such as "rage reaction," which the book introduced to them. O'Boy was so impressed that he asked Vernon Mark to appear as an expert witness for the prosecution, but Mark declined, having already discussed the case with Altschule.

In brief compass, and in terms accessible to the intelligent lay reader—though buttressed by hundreds of scientific references—Mark and Ervin proposed a theory relating human violence, and especially irrational assault, to dysfunction of the limbic system. Although they did not deny the influence of social and psychological factors, they contended that violent behavior must be regarded as "an expression of the functioning brain," and specifically of those sections of the brain known to initiate and control such actions. They went on to suggest that a great deal of "violent assaultive action," including suicides and many episodes not often classified as violence, such as automobile accidents, occurs as a manifestation of limbic disorders or temporal-lobe epilepsy, which may cause the victim to lose control over his aggressive instincts and respond to a real or imagined threat by irrational attack. Mark and Ervin labeled chronic conditions of this sort "the dyscontrol syndrome."

The men who advanced this theory were eminently respectable researchers. Sweet and Mark headed the neurosurgical services at, respectively, Massachusetts General Hospital and Boston City Hospital, two major Boston teaching hospitals. Ervin was director of the psychiatric research laboratories at Massachusetts General. All three were members of the clinical faculty of the Harvard Medical School. Their findings were based on extensive research into a serious problem that had attracted relatively little clinical attention, largely because work with violent subjects is dangerous, expensive, and disruptive to psychiatric institutions.

In applying their concept of limbic seizure to the case of Charles Decker, Mark Altschule was, characteristically, plunging into what was the hottest debate in the field of psychiatry, and probably of medical ethics as well. The focus of the storm was less Mark and Ervin's claims about the neurophysiological roots of violence than their conclusion that some deviant behavior could appropriately be treated by brain surgery.

Psychosurgery — brain surgery intended to alter behavior, to use the most neutral definition — has become controversial principally as a result of changing public attitudes. The practice itself is not new. In 1935, at the International Congress of Neurology in London, C. F. Jacobsen and J. F. Fulton of Yale University described their recent experiments on the behavioral effects of frontal-lobe lesions. Almost in passing, they mentioned that one of their monkeys had not exhibited the "experimental neurosis" that should have followed his frustration at an experimental task. Egas Moniz, a Portuguese neurologist, at once suggested that the method could be applied to relieve the distress of mentally ill humans. He quickly developed procedures for severing the frontal lobe from the thalamic nuclei, and applied them to twenty severely disturbed patients, apparently with good results. In 1936 the frontal lobotomy—and psychosurgery—came to America.

For ten years frontal lobotomy remained a rare procedure. Before 1945 there were fewer than a thousand operations, in all, in the United States. Then, suddenly, lobotomy became a medical fad. One reason for this was the urgent demand for a method of treating the flood of mentally disturbed war veterans (for the problems experienced by Vietnam veterans were less unusual than some believe). Another was the development, by Walter Freeman of George Washington University, of the transorbital technique (or "icepick method"), which enabled physicians to perform lobotomies in their offices, simply by punching a special instrument through the thin orbital bone into the brain below. In 1949 alone, five thousand frontal lobotomies were performed.

From that point on, for reasons that are not altogether clear, the popularity of the technique fell as sharply as it had risen. Clinical studies had begun to appear indicating that lobotomy had no effect on schizophrenic delusions or other thought disorders. It also became apparent that the classical frontal-lobe syndrome, marked by undue passivity, loss of initiative, and inappropriate social behavior, was a direct and unavoidable result of the therapeutic reduction of anxiety. Still, the follow-up studies also showed that lobotomy was often the only effective treatment for anxiety and depression, that it permitted the discharge of many chronically institutionalized patients, and that it caused little or no intellectual deterioration. A few lobotomy patients even resumed successful professional careers. Not until several years after the fad had passed did the introduction of antipsychotic drugs permanently relegate frontal lobotomy to use only in extreme cases and experimental procedures.

The psychosurgery advocated by Sweet, Mark, and Ervin was related to frontal lobotomy principally by analogy. They argued that the violence of the victim of temporal-lobe epilepsy or limbic disorder was comparable to the convulsions of the frontal-lobe epileptic. But the stereotactic surgery that they, and other psychosurgical groups, employ is far more sophisticated than frontal lobotomy or the temporal lobotomy traditionally used to treat extreme cases of temporal epilepsy. Stereotactic surgery, pioneered at Yale in the 1950s by the Spanish-American neurologist Jose Delgado, uses tiny electrodes implanted in the brain at the site of surgery, which destroy the cells around their tips by "burning" them (actually, the temperature generated is only about 65 degrees Celsius, or 150 degrees Fahrenheit) with a burst of high-frequency electricity. This technique allows much more precise surgery than conventional methods, with far less incidental destruction of brain tissue; moreover, the electrodes may be left in place for months, allowing the neurosurgeon to proceed cautiously both in identifying his target and in destroying it.

Stereotactic methods are essential in surgery on the areas of the brain involved in violence, because they afford access to inner portions of the brain with relatively little disturbance of surrounding tissues and because they can excise specific tiny centers rather than large structures. Thus, for example, neurosurgeons are now able to destroy specific centers in both temporal lobes, whereas a bilateral lobectomy—removal of large sections of both lobes—resulted in unacceptable alterations of brain function.

Mark and his colleagues found that they were able to control violent behavior arising from temporal-lobe epilepsy, though without curing the epilepsy itself, by destroying selected centers in the temporal lobes. They were also able to isolate particular areas of the amygdala—the small structure in front of the temporal lobe with connections to the hypothalamus—that, when stimulated electrically, initiated or stopped assaultive behavior.

Although Mark and Ervin made important contributions to the surgical treatment of violence, they were by no means alone in the field. A British neurosurgeon, M. A. Falconer, had long advocated neurological study of violent behavior, and especially its connection with temporal-lobe epilepsy. Surgery on the amygdala, the area in which the Boston group made its most important findings, was pioneered by H. Narabayashi in Japan, and introduced in the United States only after becoming relatively common in that country. Japanese culture attaches a terrible stigma to families whose children are institutionalized; as a result, the Japanese have been particularly interested in neurosurgical treatment of uncontrollable epileptic and hyper-kinetic brain-injured children. Some Japanese surgeons have moved beyond amygdalatomy and perform their "sedative surgery" directly on the hypothalamus. By 1970, bilateral amygdala destruction and other psychosurgery to control violent behavior had been carried out in many countries, and in several medical centers in America.

*

With the publication of *Violence and the Brain,* the psycho-surgery movement went public. Mark and Ervin explicitly intended their book to arouse interest in their field, in order to attract "significant financial and intellectual support" for a project, sponsored by their Neuro-Research Foundation, to establish a facility designed from the ground up and specially staffed for the study of human violence and its surgical treatment. (They were partially successful in this regard, receiv-ing a large federal research grant, though no institute.) At the same time, they expressed the hope that their book would "elicit helpful criticism" of their approach to violence.

It certainly elicited criticism. Some of this was theoretical. Despite experiments on animals and humans showing limbic control over violent behavior, and despite a growing body of solid research indicating that brain tumors, especially those affecting the limbic system, can in fact cause violence, many experts argued that there was little hard evidence to support the relationship between brain dysfunction and societal violence posited by Mark and Ervin. Some criticism was more technical, holding that the electroencephalograms (EEGs) and other measures used to locate the specific brain malfunctions to be removed were unreliable, and thus the psychosurgeon could not be sure of operating in the right place. But though the most numerous and most vociferous critics were influenced by these arguments and used them, they were primarily concerned with the moral and social implications of psychosurgery.

Psychosurgery is, by definition, surgery undertaken in order to change the behavior of the patient. (The definition does not stop there, but there is debate over its other terms.) It differs from other forms of behavior modification—psychological and psychopharmacological—in that it is apparently more drastic and irreversible, involving removal or destruction of parts of the brain. As Dr. Willard Gaylin, the psychiatrist who heads the Institute of Society, Ethics, and the Life Sciences, remarks, "psychosurgery is a prototype, at its most extreme, of all behavior modification, and suggests all the problems inherent in the other forms of behavior control."

Not surprisingly, a great deal of the criticism of psychosurgery is more emotional than rational. In part this is because there is a frightening finality about a knife or electrode excising irreplaceable brain cells. But more "acceptable" drug therapies sometimes have unexpected side effects, and these too can be irreversible. (For example, prolonged use of the antipsychotic drug chlorpromazine has been known to cause a lasting impairment of muscular control much like Parkinson's disease.) Certainly, too, we center ourselves in our heads, and that makes a difference. We can welcome heart transplants, and the implantation of artificial valves; compared to the brain, even the torso is an extremity. Yet those who speak of protecting the "organic integrity" of the brain are lost in the "mind-body problem" of the philosophers. They are actually thinking in terms of an inorganic, spiritual mind. Few would object, in theory at least, to surgical removal of visibly diseased brain tissue—a tumor, for instance—even if the purpose of the operation were to restore normal thought and behavior.

The most serious challenge to psychosurgery began with an

article published in 1971 by Dr. Peter Breggin, a Washington, D.C., psychiatrist. Breggin began by stressing the problem of diagnostic weakness in psychosurgery. His main point, however, was that this imprecision made psychosurgery, and especially techniques designed to forestall violence, susceptible to misuse as a device for the social control of dissidents. He argued that unlike somatic diseases and most psychoses, violence is an interpersonal or social phenomenon, often with political dimensions.

This was a powerful argument, especially at that particular time. The overtly political violence of the Weather Underground and Black Panthers was in the news. The idea that mental illness is an artificial concept manipulated for the control of dissidents was widely diffused by such thinkers as Thomas Szasz, R. D. Laing, and Michel Foucault. The popular cult novels, *Catch-22* and *One Flew Over the Cuckoo's Nest,* and such newer works as *The King of Hearts* and *Equus,* presented the same theme. The coincidental American publication of *A Question of Madness,* by the Soviet dissenters Zhores and Roy Medvedev, which described the use of psychiatry to isolate and "cure" political critics in the U.S.S.R., provided an object lesson in the dangers ahead.

Mark and his collaborators had tried to meet these objections beforehand by stressing that psychosurgery must remain a last resort, and that careful testing should be carried out to identify an organic focus of disease. They even adduced evidence that race riots were more or less rational responses to social conditions, and explained that their standards of "acceptable" and "unacceptable" violence applied to the police as well as to "politically activist groups." Still, there was plenty in their book, apart from its ultimate implications, to fuel the fears of critics. The authors called for an " 'early warning test' of limbic brain function" to allow identification and treatment of "potentially violent individuals," and expressed the hope that they would learn "to combat the violence-triggering mechanisms in the brains of the nondiseased."

Within four years of the publication of *Violence and the*

*Brain*, the opponents of psychosurgery had rallied strong political forces in Washington and in areas where such research was being conducted. They had aroused great concern within the medical community over the ethics and advisability of the work. And in a Detroit courtroom, they had won a ruling that a Michigan mental-hospital inmate was not a sufficiently free agent to be accepted as a voluntary participant in an amygdalatomy experiment inspired by the book.

For all his combativeness, though, Altschule was not particularly interested in the psychosurgery debate, or in the future of psychosurgery per se. From his point of view, *Violence and the Brain* was a valuable aid to diagnosis in two respects. First, it presented strong arguments, backed by extensive research, associating irrational assaultive behavior with disorders of the limbic system. Second, Mark and Ervin, in their discussion of the "dyscontrol syndrome," set forth the characteristics of a limbic attack: a sudden complete loss of control, often accompanied by irrational, unpremeditated violence, sometimes lasting an hour or more; followed by a return to normal, with horrified realization of what had happened but only fragmentary memories of the seizure itself.

This description tallied well with what Altschule had heard about Charles's assault, both from Nicholas Decker and, later, in the testimony of Gail Sussman. Moreover, he knew that this was not the first instance of abnormal behavior on his patient's part. His earlier examination of Charles, six years before, had followed a series of incidents of undue aggressiveness, culminating in the boy's attempt to pick a fight with a very large state trooper who had stopped him for drunk driving. The known episodes—and Altschule suspected there had been others dismissed as "teenage scrapes"—were associated with apparently desultory drinking. Roseman had to keep this history out of the court record because of the question of voluntary use of alcohol, but Altschule, in private, could take it into account.

Altschule's examination of the teen-age Charles Decker had proved inconclusive. Suspecting some sort of hypoglycemic attack, resulting from a depressed level of sugar in the blood, he had performed a glucose-tolerance test to trace the metabolism of that substance over time, and had studied the boy's blood for abnormal hormone levels. His only positive finding was that the presence of alcohol in Charles's bloodstream seemed to trigger an inappropriate secretion of insulin, the hormone that regulates the metabolism of glucose and other carbohydrates. This promising lead had gone nowhere, however; he could not assimilate his facts into an explanation of the situation. Now, returning to the problem with more data and a greater understanding of the effects of alcohol, he began to perceive interrelationships that he had not suspected earlier.

From the start, therefore, evidence as well as inclination directed Dr. Altschule toward a physiological interpretation of the event.

*

Ever since medicine took over from demonology the task of defining insanity, the central problem has been the relationship between mind and brain. Until the end of the nineteenth century, the dominant view was that supported by two great philosopher-scientists, Aristotle and Descartes: the mind and soul were one, the material body something separate. By one of those apparent paradoxes of intellectual history, this abstract concept of the mind led straight to a physical interpretation of insanity. The soul, ideal and immortal, must be perfect, it was believed; "mental illness" must be physical illness, actual degeneration of the brain. The frequency with which insanity followed identifiable physical disease—the paresis of syphilis was a favorite example—supported this view, as did the mental effects of brain injuries.

This theory permitted only a very limited conception of insanity, because the role it allowed the brain itself was so circumscribed. The various alternatives that were advanced over the years similarly tended to reflect the assumption that insanity was brain disease. They differed in that, in attempting to account for the observed range of mental illnesses, they assigned to the brain a greater share of mental activity. Although many of the most experienced students of insanity thus sought to broaden their profession's outlook, the dominant theory was so firmly entrenched, so tightly bound up with the general world view of the age, that their efforts were, for a long time, in vain. From time to time materialist philosophers such as Hume, La Mettrie, and d'Holbach challenged this orthodoxy, but their positions found little favor among physicians. More successful was the "science" of phrenology, developed in the early nineteenth century by the German-born anatomist Franz Joseph Gall and championed in America (for a time) by the influential medical teacher Charles Caldwell. Phrenology posited that the brain is the organ of the mind; that its various parts correspond to specific mental faculties (sometimes identifiable through the effects of brain injuries); and that the external conformation of the skull reveals the shape of the underlying brain. By feeling the "bumps" on his subject's skull, the phrenologist could, allegedly, gauge his character. Many such studies of prison inmates supposedly found overdevelopment in the areas denoting such "lower propensities" as combativeness and destructiveness. When Charles Guiteau was tried for shooting President Garfield, one Prof. A. E. Frew Mully hawked a popular pamphlet that he advertised as a "copious and correct" phrenological delineation of the assassin.

Even after phrenology went out of vogue, it left behind a surprisingly positive influence on the development of psychology. The mid-nineteenth-century concept of "moral insanity," for example, owed some of the limited acceptance it found to its pseudoscientific predecessor. This doctrine held that there were cases in which a person's emotional or moral faculties were diseased although his intellect remained unclouded. Advocated by the pioneer forensic psychiatrist Isaac Ray, moral insanity became the basis of the "irresistible impulse" insanity defense. Although the concept won the support of many leading psychiatrists (or alienists, as they were then called), including McLean superintendents Luther V. Bell and John E. Tyler, it eventually succumbed in most courts to the stricter M'Naghten rule, and in the medical profession to the old idealism.

*

Darwinian evolution, which asserted man's place in the natural world, was a powerful challenge to old orthodoxies in every sphere of biological science. According to Cesare Lombroso, an Italian psychologist and asylum director, most of those classified as criminally insane, and some forty percent of all criminals, were in fact throwbacks down the evolutionary ladder whose sociopathic behavior arose from a lack of human moral faculties. Such criminals, he insisted, could be identified not only by their bestial acts but also by atavistic physical traits revealing their kinship with apes, wolves, or flounders. Lombroso was a penal reformer who hoped that his work would promote understanding of these unfortunates and lead to better treatment of them. His ideas were widely influential, but, in practice, they tended to brand the criminally insane as incurably vicious, and thus worked against humane treatment.

Lombroso also noted the similarity of some criminal assaults to epileptic seizures. This idea was taken up by a number of American psychologists, and one of them, Edward C. Mann, coined the term *moral epilepsy* to describe a disorder of the central nervous system resulting in recurrent but temporary criminal impulses. Mann believed, too, that certain kinds of alcoholism associated with early degeneration of brain centers were a form of insanity, and should be admissible as a defense in criminal trials. Thus, well before the end of the nineteenth century, recognized leaders of the American psychiatric community were taking positions suggestive of those Altschule would support almost a hundred years later.

In the interim, however, the old orthodox view that insanity must be a manifestation of physical dysfunction was swept away and replaced by a second, opposite attitude. This second great wave of thought was the psychogenic outlook, which has dominated medicine during most of the twentieth century. According to this theory, most cases of mental illness are caused by purely psychological or emotional factors—traumatic experiences or failures of personality development. Just as the physicalist view of insanity was associated with the concept of an ideal mind-soul, the psychogenic view derived, genetically if not logically, from a materialist understanding of the human mind.

Its founding father was, of course, Sigmund Freud, though from the start there were challenges and heresies against his authority within the broader movement. Freud, a neurologist by training, began his work with studies of the physical brain, and proceeded through clinical investigations of mental illness to the development of psychoanalytic theory.

The psychoanalytic approach offered valuable insights into many spheres of human life, from psychiatry to literature. Unfortunately, its predominance tended to overwhelm alternative ways of understanding, even when these had already proved their usefulness. Studies of genetic influence on mental state, and of correlations between physical and psychic characteristics — once important areas of research — almost came to a halt. Even in purely psychological fields, the new orthodoxy could limit horizons. For example, Freudians placed so much emphasis on the child's relationship with his parents that for thirty years the role of peer relationships — friendships — in personality development was ignored.

In criminal insanity, as in other forms of mental illness, psychogenic interpretations were widely adduced. A person who killed women might be acting out unresolved conflicts with his mother, while a sociopath's condition might be attributed to an impoverished background and disturbed home life. Though this became the standard sort of psychiatric testimony in the courtroom, its nature encouraged long-standing doubts about the validity of the insanity defense. Compared to physical medical evidence, this seemed subjective and theoretical. Besides, many factors to which psychiatrists ascribed insanity sounded, to laymen, more like excuses than causes of actual illness.

So pervasive was Freudianism, and the psychogenic interpretation of insanity generally, within the psychiatric profession, that emotional causes were sought even for mental conditions whose physical etiology was well established. For several decades, relatively little research was conducted on the physical roots of mental illness.

Interest in the physical causes of mental phenomena never disappeared altogether, however. There was always a handful of neurologists, pharmacologists, and other specialists who remained concerned with the question. Though the Freudian heyday coincided with American predominance in medical research, there were other countries where its influence was less pervasive. One of these was the Soviet Union. Marxist materialism was naturally unsympathetic to Freud's thought, and it was reinforced by a prerevolutionary Russian tradition of biological psychiatry, of which Korsakoff was an exemplar. Besides, Russia was the home of the most important competing psychogenic theory, the Pavlovian school that emphasized conditioned response. While Soviet psychiatry is notoriously politicized, much of the best work on cerebral function has been done in the U.S.S.R.

Moreover, it must be understood that modern psychogenic theories do not deny the ultimate importance of the functioning physical brain, they merely ignore it. Freudians may talk and reason as if the ego, superego, and id are Platonic ideals distinct from anatomical reality, but that is not their theoretical position. Some may hold a religious belief in the soul, but, scientifically, they accept a materialist view of the mind. Or consider Arthur Janov's primal therapy, a fad of the early 1970s, in which patients are encouraged to scream in order to free themselves of repressed traumatic memories. What could be a clearer example of a purely psychogenic theory of mental disturbance and psychotherapy? Yet in Janov's therapy those "primal screams" are screams of real, physical pain, indicating (and releasing) real "knots" in the brain that physically encode those memories.

The popularity of primal therapy, however short-lived, is one of many signs that the hegemony of psychogenic theories of psychology is passing. Not that psychogenic theory is disappearing. Rather, it is fragmenting into more and more schools and eclectic movements, of which Janov's is only one. "Psychobabble," to use R. D. Rosen's term, is the order of the day. It is difficult today to define a psychiatric mainstream. Orthodox Freudian psychoanalysis has become almost a rarity, as other movements, neo-Freudian and non-Freudian, arise.

There is also a rekindled interest in the Pavlovian tradition of conditioned response; behavior modification is being used not only to control habits such as smoking and overeating but also, with some success, to treat more serious psychiatric problems. In prepared childbirth—the Lamaze method—the mother-to-be is conditioned to relax as she follows certain breathing patterns, thus lessening her perception of labor pain. This Pavlovian system, though introduced to this country from France, is, not surprisingly, a refinement of a Russian technique. Recently, defense psychiatrists in criminal cases have begun to make use of such concepts as the "Stockholm syndrome" and the "Vietnam syndrome," which are essentially based on conditioning theory.

At the same time, there is renewed interest in physical causes of mental disturbance. The psychiatric implications of discoveries in such fields as endocrinology and genetics have become too obvious to ignore. The most striking and best-known instance of the success of biopsychiatry (the treatment of mental illness as a biological problem) involves schizophrenia. This condition, called dementia praecox in earlier times, suggests split personality to most laymen, but in fact that is just one of its many manifestations, and an uncommon one at that. Schizophrenia can be defined only in general terms, as a separation of the intellectual from the emotional processes, or of the self from reality. In its many guises, it dominated professional and public perceptions of insanity for more than a century. The stock caricature of the lunatic with his hand thrust into his vest, convinced he is Napoleon Bonaparte, is a schizophrenic. So were the ranting, screaming inmates who filled mental wards up to the middle of this century, giving our language the words *madhouse* and *bedlam* (the latter from the popular name for Bethlehem Hospital, London's first asylum).

Schizophrenia was seized upon by advocates of psychogenic interpretations of insanity as a prime example of a condition brought about by purely psychological forces. The nature of its manifestations—dreaminess, separation from reality, delusions, hallucinations, megalomania, and paranoia, as well as the famous split personality—certainly suggested that it could best be understood in psychological terms. Besides, despite a few suggestions that the condition might be inherited, there was no known association with physical causes, and no sign that it had any existence except on the psychical level. Psychiatrists did not agree on its exact etiology—Freud and Jung attributed it to buried complexes, while Alfred Meyer saw it as the result of a series of personality maladaptations—but they did agree that it should be understood and treated (though treatment was impossible in many cases) in psychological terms.

Then, shortly after the Second World War, a new treatment appeared. Chlorpromazine was a synthetic antihistamine that didn't work very well in fighting allergic reactions, but its calming effect on those who took it caught the attention of a French psychiatrist, Pierre Deniker. When he tried it on acute schizophrenics, he found that it was remarkably effective in controlling their symptoms, even in some cases that had been regarded as beyond hope.

His discovery, and the further advances that ensued, constitute the greatest revolution in mental-health care in modern times. As a result of the widespread use of antipsychotic drugs, thousands of patients who a generation ago would have been incapacitated by mental illness are now able to function quite normally, and many more have been freed from asylums and are treated as outpatients. Today in the United States, the average period of hospitalization for mental patients, and the number of institutionalized patients at any given time, are less than half of what they were as recently as the early 1960s. Within twenty years, the proportion of mental patients being treated on an outpatient basis has risen from under a quarter to more than two-thirds. This rapid deinstitutionalization of the mentally ill has not been an unmixed success. Because of insufficient support facilities (halfway houses, for example) for these outpatients, and because many, though no longer in need of constant supervision, still lack the ability to function normally and productively in the outside world, released mental patients have come to form a new class of derelicts on the streets of American cities, often outnumbering the long-established wino population. Nevertheless, from a medical point of view antipsychotics have been a resounding success.

This did not mean, however, that physicians understood how their new wonder drug worked. When researchers investigated this question, they found that chlorpromazine and its cousins seemed to stimulate certain cells within the brain that secrete dopamine, a chemical known to be involved in the transmission of neural impulses. Nonetheless, the mechanism remained obscure, for the drugs did not seem to affect these cells directly. The explanation proved to be a hitherto-unsuspected feedback system that controlled the brain's neural function. Antipsychotic drugs were found to act on postsynaptic receptor cells, cells that ordinarily receive the dopamine released by cells in the presynaptic membrane. Because the chemical structure of the drugs resembled that of dopamine in some respects, they could "impersonate" dopamine well enough to block the receptor sites; then the feedback mechanism came into play, registering the fact that "real" dopamine was not being received, and therefore stimulating the presynaptic cells to release more of it.

Further research uncovered more far-reaching aspects of the neurochemical system, of which the dopamine-controlled synapses turned out to be just one element. Other neural pathways utilizing other chemical transmitters were identified. Each of these pathways was found to have more than one function, and to be susceptible to more than one type of malfunction. The dopamine pathway controlled not only mental functions but also certain aspects of muscular coordination. L-Dopa and other drugs used to treat Parkinson's disease also act on the dopamine pathway, but their effect is the reverse of the antipsychotics', for they suppress the secretion of the chemical. Parkinson's patients on L-Dopa sometimes exhibit psychotic side effects, while schizophrenics receiving heavy doses of antipsychotic drugs may develop muscular-coordination problems.

Though chemical treatment of schizophrenia, the commonest form of psychosis, was the most spectacular success of biopsychiatry, it was not the only one. Lithium treatment for depression, though less well understood, narrowly predated the introduction of chlorpromazine. Moreover, while Altschule was considering the puzzle of Charles Decker's condition, another breakthrough in neurochemistry was transforming scientists' views of how the brain works. This was the discovery of a whole new chemical system within the brain, based on endorphins, "natural opiates" (whose chemistry is mimicked by narcotics, just as dopamine's is by antipsychotics) that apparently have a role in controlling the emotions as well as suppressing pain.

Meanwhile, geneticists too had been investigating mental illness. By studying families with unusually high incidences of schizophrenia, they were able to conclude that that condition was the result, in at least some cases, of multifactorial genetic inheritance. That is, they concluded that the disease was brought about by a linking of several minor gene abnormalities, perhaps in combination with environmental factors. This concept of a genetic (or other physical) predisposition to psychogenic disturbance may represent a fruitful accommodation of the two major approaches to mental illness.

All of this supported Altschule's ideas about the ultimate nature of mental illness, for throughout his career he had been committed to the belief that it was predominantly a physical phenomenon. Now, for the first time, the tide seemed to be turning in his direction. His position in the flow of medical opinion about mental illness was somewhat analogous to David Roseman's sense of his own place in the legal evolution of the concept. Roseman believed he detected in recent court opinions a willingness to give greater weight to a defendant's claim of insanity, particularly if it was supported by physical evidence. Even if he lost at the trial, the lawyer felt that the Supreme Judicial Court might be poised to establish a new precedent on appeal. The physician, too, knew that in his own profession the climate of opinion about mental illness was changing, and that this attitudinal shift offered an opportunity to open new frontiers in the struggle against disease. In the case of Charles Decker he too saw an opportunity to influence history.

*

"We needed a poison," says Altschule, "a poison that could be generated during the breakdown of alcohol." From the start, the physician had a pretty good idea of what he was looking for. The study of the interplay of alcohol and the mind is one of those fields in which psychogenic theory long predominated. Much research was directed at understanding the psychic forces that drove men and women to drink, and at delineating the "alcoholic personality." At the same time, the ways in which alcohol consumption affected the mind were generally ignored. Studies revealed, for example, that drinkers involved in crimes of violence were usually not alcoholics but acutely intoxicated nonalcoholics, yet none of these same studies considered the psychological relationship of alcoholism to violence. Altschule, of course, rejected facile psychiatric assumptions. Moreover, he had considerable evidence that in Charles Decker's case at least, the link between alcohol and assault was physical. On the basis of behavioral evidence, principally the victims' testimony, he had diagnosed a limbic seizure. With the discovery of Korsakoff's syndrome, he had a definite indication of physical damage to the limbic system. Both the syndrome's etiology and the particular circumstances of the attack suggested that alcohol was somehow involved. Charles's history of inappropriate insulin secretion tied in with both unusual metabolism of alcohol and neurological damage, and reinforced Altschule's predisposition toward an endocrinological explanation. Altschule did not yet know how the pieces of the jigsaw would fit together, but he was beginning to discern the shape, at least, of the finished puzzle.

The physician even suspected that he could name the poison he was after. Years before, he recalled, his onetime Harvard colleague Wilfred W. Westerfield (later professor of biochemistry at the State University of New York's Upstate Medical Center) had found that when some people metabolize alcohol, their bodies produce an abnormal chemical by-product: 2,3-butanediol. Chemically, butanediol is closely related to acetaldehyde, the principal breakdown product of ethyl alcohol, which is present in the bloodstream of anyone who drinks.

The butanediol molecule consists of a four-unit chain of carbon atoms (the "butane") linking two alcohol radicals (signified by the "diol"). It occurs in several forms, each having the same atomic constituents, but distinguished by where on the carbon chain the alcohol radicals are attached. In 1,3-butanediol, they are on the first and third carbons; in 2,3-butanediol, on the second and third. The former, though not a normal metabolite, has been used as a carbohydrate supplement in animal feed and, experimentally, in human diets; except for a narcotic effect when administered in enormous doses, 1,3-butanediol apparently poses no danger. But the shift of a single chemical bond produces 2,3-butanediol, which is toxic to human brain tissue.

Nicholas Decker provided an additional suggestion about the genesis of his son's seizure. A colleague with whom he had discussed the case had raised the possibility that adrenalin (epinephrine), the hormone that increases the heart rate and other physiological functions in times of stress, might be implicated. It was certainly reasonable to assume that adrenalin would be present in a situation of excitation, fear, or perceived threat that might lead to an attack. Moreover, one effect of adrenalin in the bloodstream is to increase the rate of metabolism of blood sugar; thus it could reinforce the effect of an oversupply of insulin.

Mark Altschule insists that medical research must be guided by clinical observation, not by preconceived theory. He deplores the "scientific" tendency to theorize—"Many of my academic colleagues are great athletes," he remarks, "they're great at leaping to conclusions"—and considers it absurd that scholars must cite "expected results" in applying for research grants, and advance hypothetical explanations when submitting their findings for publication. Nevertheless, he admits that in the case of Charles Decker he started out, as everyone must, with "certain assumptions," themselves derived from clinical observation. But he refuses to concede that his speculations about the origin and nature of Charles's condition constituted a guiding hypothesis for his tests. His only theory, he maintains, was that the incident could be reproduced in the laboratory.

In late March of 1975, Altschule set out to re-create the conditions that had, eight months before, turned Charles Decker into a raging beast. Though he believed that the seizure of July

17 had come about as a result of the interplay of several factors, only two were under his control: alcohol and adrenalin. His procedure seemed straightforward. He would administer alcohol intravenously to his patient, and monitor the results by direct observation and by taking blood samples over the following hours and days. Then the test would be repeated, this time with the addition of epinephrine.

Blood feeds the human brain. It is the agent of its respiration and nutrition. The brain uses a quarter of the body's oxygen and expends a tenth of its energy. Among the other external influences transmitted to the brain through the bloodstream are medicines, narcotics, and alcohol, which is broken down in the blood into other compounds. The blood also carries the hormones, such as adrenalin, that are secreted into it by the endocrine glands. Both Altschule and Decker had extensive backgrounds in endocrinology, though of rather different sorts.

There were two things that could go wrong with Altschule's attempt to reproduce the chemical trigger that had set off Charles's attack. The experiment could fail, leaving Altschule in the dark about his patient's behavior. Or it could succeed, and put a madman on his hands. Fortunately, Shattuck was a prison hospital, and its staff was used to handling violent patients. They received with gratifying equanimity the physician's warning that his so far well-behaved patient might go berserk in the middle of the test. They were, he was assured, quite prepared to deal with that eventuality.

It did not arise. Altschule administered the alcohol, the equivalent of five to six highballs, over the span of an hour. (For some reason, in such studies on the effect of alcohol, volume is traditionally expressed in terms of highballs, a term that dates the early research to a time when people drove beach wagons and played canasta.) More precisely, Altschule injected 100 milliliters, or almost three and a half ounces, of pure ethyl alcohol. Charles showed absolutely no reaction to this laboratory equivalent of a bout of heavy drinking. Whatever the effect of alcohol metabolism on his limbic brain, he surely had, in conventional terms, a good head for liquor. Altschule was somewhat surprised at this very high tolerance, though it did seem to confirm that ordinary drunkenness was not the young man's problem. Altschule completed the first series by extracting blood from the other arm at intervals after concluding the administration of the alcohol. The second experiment, in which adrenalin was administered along with the alcohol, similarly caused no behavioral change. If the tests had produced any useful results, they would have to be found in laboratory analysis of the blood samples.

When Altschule saw the assay findings, he was not encouraged. He hoped, however, that Nicholas Decker would find something in the figures that he had missed. The two men had known each other for almost forty years, since Decker, a young biochemist, had come to Boston's Beth Israel Hospital (where Altschule was to become director of research) to set up a sterility laboratory. Now, Altschule served as a consultant to the Office of Naval Research facility where his friend conducted blood research. Throughout their long relationship, Altschule had been the clinician, Decker the laboratory experimenter.

When Altschule brought him the assay results, Decker ran an experienced eye over them and pronounced, "These stink." The figures, he told his friend, did not show that Charles was normal or abnormal; they did not show anything at all. "Mark had done a routine hospital procedure," he recalls, "and the numbers were a bunch of baloney." The test would have to be repeated, he told Altschule, and "this time I'm running the lab end. I'll time it, and you leave the specimen timing, the infusion, and so on to me." He set about searching among his long-time associates in hospital diagnostic laboratories for someone who could perform adequate assays, preferably without demanding immediate payment, for legal expenses were mounting. The tests could not be run for several weeks, in any case, because his son had to be allowed time to regenerate the pint of blood lost in the course of the first procedure.

Meanwhile, there were other tests that Altschule wanted to perform. The simplest of these was an ordinary electroenceph-alogram, a recording of electrical discharges in the brain (brain waves) using external monitors attached to the scalp. This could not uncover dysfunctions deep in the limbic system, but it might show that a lesion in the outer cortex was involved in triggering the limbic attack — a condition known as psychomotor epilepsy. This routine procedure was performed without difficulty in the Shattuck facilities, but the results, not unexpectedly, were negative.

Apparently the dysfunction, if detectable, was limited to the limbic area itself. Short of opening the skull, which was out of the question, that region of the brain was accessible to electrodes only by the use of nasopharyngeal leads introduced through the nasal passages to reach the base of the brain; and even this approach was not altogether reliable. Altschule asked the Shattuck physicians about the possibility of conducting such a test in their laboratory, but they told him that their experience with the procedure had been discouraging, and that they were unwilling to undertake it in Charles's case.

A second method by which a limbic lesion might be located was CAT-scan (computerized axial tomography). This technique couples an extremely sensitive x-ray machine with a computerized imaging process to produce "cross-sections" of the body, showing not just bones but soft tissues as well, with their tumors and other malformations. On the basis of his knowledge of Wernicke-Korsakoff disease, Altschule suspected that even this most sophisticated of modern diagnostic tools would not detect Charles's problem, because the condition tended to manifest itself as a spotty lesion — a large number of tiny flaws rather than a single large hole that would register on the CAT-scanner. The point was moot, for the time being at least. CAT-scanning was a brand-new technology and a very expensive one, available at only a few hospitals, Shattuck not among them. Transferring Charles for the purpose of making such a reading raised the same problems as had the plan to take him to McLean, and, in addition, the CAT-scan facilities of general hospitals were much less secure than a mental hospital. Since the physician doubted that a conclusive finding was likely, he decided that the test was not worth the effort.

By early May, both Charles Decker and his father were ready for the second series of endocrinological assays. Nicholas Decker was taking a considerable risk with his son's future, though he apparently did not know it. In his own view, he was a scrupulous scientist performing an objective test to arrive at precise medical findings. He ignored the legal aspect of the situation: the fact that key evidence in his own son's criminal trial, developed in part by him, would pass through his hands for testing by his friends. Perhaps David Roseman should have alerted him to the danger, but the lawyer thought of the test as Altschule's — which it was — and may not have realized how much Decker had taken upon himself. Certainly Frank O'Boy, who could have used this fact in court to impugn the credibility of the tests, was unaware of it. The prosecutor did not even know that Altschule, the defense's expert witness, was an old friend of the defendant's father.

Decker was hardly indifferent to his son's fate. He had thrown himself into the case from the start, in both its legal and its medical aspects, and had already run up bills of more than $10,000 in the defense effort. Yet however sincere his underlying paternal feelings, he assumed a demeanor of scientific detachment that others could easily perceive as coldness. He could decline to bail Charles out of prison, and even remark that the tests might confirm that his son should be an inmate for life; but at the same time he could be outraged by what he saw as sloppy laboratory procedure. The young man himself was not even aware of his father's scientific role in his defense. "If you ever wanted to see a startled boy, you should have seen my son," recalls Nicholas Decker, "because this was down behind bars, you see, and he came out of the hospital ward and saw me standing there — Mark he could accept, but not his father."

This time, of course, the testing proceeded like clockwork. Again the Corrections Department guards were warned that their charge might become violent; and again he exhibited little response to the alcohol. A laboratory assistant, not Nicholas Decker, administered the alcohol and the epinephrine in one arm, and drew the fourteen blood samples (one before administration, six afterward, in each series) from the other, but Decker controlled the timing and labeled the samples with scientific precision.

He then took the samples halfway across town to the Pratt Diagnostic Clinic, a specialized analytical service of the Tufts – New England Medical Center. Decker had served on the Pratt staff more than thirty years before, and he still had old colleagues there who were prepared to help him out and would let him pay when he could. Here the blood samples would be analyzed by laboratory scientists using the best standard techniques. The procedure they chose was enzymatic analysis. An enzyme is an organic catalyst that, remaining unchanged itself, accelerates chemical reactions that break down certain other organic compounds. Each enzyme facilitates the breakdown of a defined range of chemically related substances, without affecting others. If the analyst has some idea of what he expects to find, he can select the appropriate enzyme to break down and isolate the target substance. In this case, the target substance was alcohol, and the Pratt diagnosticians found it.

They identified it in the first postadministration sample, in a concentration of 250 milligrams per hundred cubic centimeters of blood, and continued to find it in declining concentrations throughout the day. This was normal. But they also found alcohol, or some alcohol-like substance, in the sample drawn the next morning *before* the second administration. By all known rules of alcohol metabolism, the residue should have disappeared from Charles's system within ten to twelve hours; yet this reading showed a level of 35 milligrams of the alcohol-like substance, twenty-two hours later. "Labs always come back with the wrong numbers," remarked Altschule, with the cynicism of the experienced clinician. "I know that," returned Decker. "But not this time, buddy."

*

Decker was convinced that the discovery of this freakish residue meant that the case was broken; yet, though the result was encouraging, it did not represent much of a conceptual advance beyond the researchers' preliminary surmise that something unusual was going on in Charles Decker's metabolism of alcohol. They still had no mechanism to explain the effects they had observed, and, more important, no evidence to link their findings with irrational violent behavior. They did not even know what the mysteriously persistent substance in Charles's bloodstream was. The enzyme that was used in the analysis is by no means specific for ethyl alcohol; it acts on a large number of related chemical compounds, many of which—including Altschule's guess, butanediol—are known to occur in the human body.

A more precise analysis was called for, and that meant gas chromatography. Anyone who has watched television shows such as *Quincy* is familiar with the gas chromatograph—the large beige machine in the corner that ostensibly permits technicians to glance at a readout and exclaim, "Doc, look at this. That cocoa contained the venom of a rare South American tree snake, at least twice the fatal dose." Gas chromatography is good, but not that good. As Altschule says, "The idea that you just do a test and get an answer, that's nonsense." The new analysis did not identify any unknown substance in Charles's blood, and was not intended to. What it did was measure, more precisely and specifically than the enzymatic approach, the concentrations of the known substance, ethyl alcohol. But when the findings of the two analyses were charted together, Altschule and Decker found a broad gap between the two curves. In every specimen, the enzyme analysis revealed more alcohol-like substance than the gas chromatograph found alcohol. In the first sample, taken at the end of the intravenous administration, about a third of the "alcohol" in the bloodstream proved to be something else. The next morning, the actual alcohol was, as orthodoxy predicted, virtually gone, and the perplexing residue was the unknown material.

Nothing in the published scientific literature about alcohol metabolism suggested that such a result was possible. Both Altschule and Decker were now working far from their own areas of expertise, and, faced with this novel situation, they were somewhat at a loss about how to proceed. "Well," said the physiologist, "who in hell knows alcohol metabolism better than the books?" His colleague suggested Richard L. Veech, a physician and biochemist who had participated in the most recent symposium on the pineal gland. Veech, then a research biochemist with the National Institute of Mental Health (NIMH) and now head of the metabolism laboratory at NIMH's Institute for Alcohol Abuse and Addiction, was in touch with the latest research on alcohol throughout the world. Decker was traveling to Washington, so he decided to search him out.

When the expert saw Decker's figures, he shook his head and said, "Can't be." It turned out that he was not simply expressing orthodox preconceptions. His institution, he explained, had tested blood from more than a dozen patients, using both methods of analysis, and—he showed Decker his own numbers—had found no discrepancies. His people, he admitted, had not run full-scale tolerance tests in these patients following the metabolism of alcohol over time. But even after Decker stressed the precision with which he had conducted the tests on his son, Veech remained skeptical. Finally, he suggested that Altschule and Decker try to reproduce their results, but this time administer the alcohol orally. This procedure would more accurately reflect real-life conditions, and the different course of the alcohol through the body might yield different results.

Decker's confidence that he and Altschule had indeed documented a metabolic abnormality in his son was not shaken by Veech's doubts. If anything, learning that the best-informed scholar in the field had never encountered such a phenomenon heightened his own conviction that they were on the trail of something new and important. Decker was prepared to accede to the suggestion of further studies, however, both because reproducibility is the test of an experiment's validity, and because they had so much more to learn about Charles's condition.

On the other hand, Veech's proposal called for a longer period of even more careful observation than had the earlier tests, under conditions more difficult to achieve in the prison hospital.

Altschule was enthusiastic about the proposal, but he wanted to run the new series at the Beth Israel Hospital, a major teaching hospital of the Harvard Medical School, where he had long been a staff member. Although the courts had authorized Charles's transfer first to McLean and then to Shattuck, it was unrealistic to expect a judge to allow a prisoner awaiting trial for attempted murder to be moved to an ordinary general hospital.

Altschule's reexamination of Charles solved the problem. The physician saw his patient at Shattuck and ran through the Korsakoff's test again. This time, he was able to detect no memory deficit whatever: the young man's mental function appeared perfectly normal. He could not conclude that the brain lesions had healed entirely, but evidently ten months of imprisonment, with no alcohol except that administered in the tests, had effectively cured the disease (as indeed Altschule's own study had shown that it could). Decker, reassured by Altschule's assessment and eager to pursue the further research, decided to take the step he had refused to take for so long and bail his son out.

On the strength of Altschule and Decker's findings, David Roseman petitioned the court to reduce the $50,000 bail, but was refused. Nicholas Decker and his wife pledged their Rehoboth farm as security for the full amount, and Charles was released from custody on July 15, 1975 — three days short of a year after his surrender.

Whatever relief the young man felt was quickly tempered by new legal problems. His wife Pamela served him with separation papers — a prelude to divorce — demanding custody of their child, financial support, and protection from any restraint on her personal liberty. Her petition noted that her husband had been "arrested and charged with the brutal assault of two young girls" and that he had been confined at the "Massachusetts Correctional Institute, at Bridgewater, for the criminally and sexually dangerous, for psychiatric examination." Up to this point, the complaint merely repeated matters of public record, albeit in the lurid detail typical of the divorce court.

But Charles's wife went further, contending that before his

arrest he "did engage in excessive consumption of alcohol beverages" and marijuana. The complaint alluded to his "propensity for violence" and claimed he might be drug-dependent. All the legal problems David Roseman had anticipated might be raised by the Massachusetts rule on voluntary consumption of alcohol threatened to come tumbling out. Charles's parents had stood steadfastly behind him, financing his defense, providing his bail, and now, on his release, opening their home to him and his daughter. His wife, on the other hand, seemed unconcerned that her attempt to regain custody of their daughter Rosamond might send the child's father to jail.

Two weeks after his release from prison, Charles Decker returned to the Shattuck Hospital for a third alcohol-tolerance test. This time only one set of blood samples was taken, to allow more rapid recovery in time for the next tests. The goal of the experiment, therefore, was simply to discover whether the abnormal persistence of the alcohol-like substance, as measured by enzymatic analysis, would recur.

It did. Not only did the blood-alcohol readings continue to climb for an hour after intravenous administration ended, but significant levels of the mysterious substance were recorded more than twenty-four hours later. The researchers had confirmed that Charles's alcohol metabolism was abnormal. Now it was time to identify the unknown substance.

The next month, Charles Decker was admitted to Beth Israel Hospital, where Altschule's friendship with the staff, many of whom were members of his network of former students, had won him full cooperation. This time, following Veech's suggestion, a somewhat different kind of test was planned. Charles would drink the alcohol, rather than receive it intravenously. A 100-milliliter dose, mixed into twelve ounces of Tab (the low-calorie soft drink) would be served to him each morning for three days, and tolerance tests would be conducted throughout the period.

Right away, something unexpected happened — unexpected, that is, on the basis of the previous tests. Charles got drunk. The "very high tolerance" for alcohol that Altschule had observed in the past seemed to have disappeared. As the young man drank the Tab cocktail over a span of forty minutes, he became noticeably tipsy, as most people would if they started drinking highballs at eight in the morning. On the second day, the results were spectacular. After finishing the drink, Charles suddenly became very ill.

"I've been in experimental medicine for many years," says Altschule, "and it's never been my policy to be away from a patient's side during any test or experiment." He was glad he had stayed with this patient, though he did not like what he was seeing. Charles was pale and sweating, mentally confused and physically uncoordinated. Altschule's first reaction, based on his bedside experience, was that his patient was in critical condition: "I was convinced that I'd killed him." On second thought, he realized that with all the facilities of a modern hospital at hand, he should be able to cope with any eventuality. "With present methods, it's almost impossible to kill anybody any more," he says. Still, he knew that each new dose of alcohol should cause a more pronounced reaction. That had been the basis of the experiment's design, and the results so far had borne out that expectation. He canceled the third day of tests. Charles still felt ill, though less so, the next morning; he was not released from the hospital until noon on the fourth day.

Altschule initially concluded that he had given his subject too much alcohol, too fast. Then, looking over his records, he noted another factor that could have contributed to Charles's sharp reaction to the alcohol: he had drunk it on an empty stomach. The young man had skipped breakfast each day, and in the course of the two days of completed tests had eaten only one meal, at five o'clock of the first afternoon. If this was his habitual eating pattern—and the physician quickly ascertained that it was—it could have important implications. One point on which all alcohol researchers agree is that the only specific for its effects is food. Here scientists merely confirm the lore of bartenders, whose secret elixirs are concocted to insinuate nourishment into mutinous systems. Because of the insulin abnormality that he had discovered years before, Altschule from the start had expected to find that unusual levels of, or utilization of, blood sugar were involved in his patient's condition. Obviously, a person who ate very irregularly, and frequently went most of a day without taking any food, would often experience abnormally low blood-sugar levels, even without inappropriate insulin secretion—which, by promoting the needless consumption of blood sugar, would exacerbate the effect.

The Beth Israel test, though cut short, was not altogether inconclusive. A considerable amount of the "unknown" was found in blood specimens drawn over the three-day period, including, as before, those taken long after the alcohol should have cleared Charles's system. This repetition of the earlier results, obtained under different circumstances, was further confirmation that Veech's skepticism about the phenomenon was unwarranted. Equally important, a sample of the mysterious substance collected in this test was set aside for analysis by an ultrasensitive gas chromatograph at a commercial testing laboratory. This was a time-consuming process, but it would finally enable Altschule and Decker to name the unidentified fluid.

Similar tests, administered under somewhat different conditions (for example, the alcohol was mixed with orange juice), only confused matters. Again Charles became drunk, but this time there was no unknown substance. Altschule did not regard this as a significant setback, however, because there was already sufficient evidence of abnormality. Besides, there was no reason to expect that whatever dysfunction was at work would operate at all times. (Indeed, it might be advantageous to the legal defense to have evidence of such unpredictability.)

Meanwhile, both Altschule and Decker continued to study the scientific literature and consult with fellow researchers, seeking additional information to guide their own work. One interesting fact they learned was that in a study of blood samples drawn from arrested criminals for police purposes, testing by both enzymatic and chromatographic methods had revealed similar discrepant readings in four percent of the cases. They also found that at the Downstate Medical Center in Brooklyn, New York, Dr. Milton M. Gross and his associates, who were studying acute alcohol-withdrawal syndrome, had, apparently inadvertently, induced an alcohol-triggered limbic attack. After receiving alcohol, one of their patients had become so violent that the experiment had to be ended. Afterward, he was "deeply ashamed and contrite," and explained, "When I drink on the outside, I try to drink it down so fast that I pass right out. When I come to, I do the same again." Only thus could he avoid involvement in a succession of violent assaults. Gross noted, too, that this subject tended to eat poorly.

Roseman obtained another continuance from the court, and Altschule made arrangements to take Charles Decker to Brooklyn. There, in mid-November, a series of tests was conducted using Gross's specialized facilities. For three consecutive nights, the young man's EEG was recorded, and blood samples and breathalyzer readings were taken periodically to test for alcohol. Alcohol, however, was not administered. The brain waves revealed no residual brain damage of the sort Gross had found in some of his patients. The breath analysis, too, was negative. But once again enzyme analysis of the blood samples found alcohol, or something like it, where the chromatograph did not—and where there should have been none.

*

Altschule's research was progressing. On the basis of the tests he had conducted since Charles's release on bail, he had gained an increasingly detailed understanding of his patient's condition. He had learned that the young man's eating habits might play a role in the problem, that the method by which alcohol was administered made a difference, and that the unexpected alcoholic residue might appear even when Charles had taken no alcohol. Soon, he hoped, he would know (though he already had his suspicions) what the unidentified substance was.

In other, perhaps more important respects, however, he still knew very little. He did not know where the unknown material came from, how it was produced, or even what it was. He could not tell what effect it had on his patient's brain, or whether it could have caused his crime. Finally—and as a physician this was always important to him—he could not suggest any treatment for the condition, except to deny Charles alcohol and encourage him to eat regularly; and he could not offer any definite prognosis even if this regimen were followed.

Yet the most recent court order, the one that had permitted the Brooklyn tests, had carried the proviso that no further continuances would be allowed. It was time to go to trial, and the defense would have to go with what it had.

What the defense had in April 1976 was, essentially, what it had had in May 1975: research in progress. It had behavioral evidence, in the form of the victims' testimony describing the events of the night of the crime. It had a diagnosis of Korsakoff's syndrome, an organic dysfunction of the limbic system generally induced by alcohol. And it had the results of the blood assays indicating that there was something definitely abnormal about Charles Decker's alcohol metabolism. But it had no demonstrable causal links to tie this together; it relied on the controversial theories of *Violence and the Brain*.

Lawyers are accustomed to dealing with science in finished form. The laws of ballistics, for example, have been well established since the seventeenth century and are not subject to frequent revision. So Mark Altschule and Nicholas Decker were not merely faced with presenting new scientific facts. They felt they also had to teach the legal system to understand science as a process, so that the court could decide that though the work was not yet complete, its direction was sound and its preliminary findings justified continuing the research. "First," says Decker, "we had to educate David—which was one hell of a job." Then Roseman, with Altschule's help, had to educate the court.

# 5. Trial

BEFORE *Commonwealth v. Decker* was called for trial, Judge Thomas Dwyer beckoned the lawyers to the bench for an off-the-record conference. Dwyer asked David Roseman what kind of defense he had prepared. Criminal irresponsibility, the lawyer answered. "He gave me a quizzical look," remembers Roseman, "as if to say, 'You're no kid and you've been around, and I'm no kid and I've been around.' He didn't say it, but that was the sense of the look."

Dwyer's skepticism was hardly surprising. The insanity defense is never easy to establish, and this defendant had already been found sane and competent to stand trial by a state-hospital staff. It was crucial for the defense to allay the judge's doubts, as Dwyer alone would determine Charles Decker's guilt or innocence. For over a year the defense had struggled with the ticklish question of whether it wanted to exercise its constitutional right to a trial by jury. It was not only a matter of who would decide Charles's fate—a panel of twelve citizens, or a single judge— but also of how the defense would present its case.

Technically, the decision to waive the jury rests with the defendant alone, and Judge Dwyer did question Charles to verify that he understood what he was doing, but obviously such an important strategic choice is made only in consultation with a lawyer. Roseman, protecting his client's confidences, will not reveal the specific advice he gave, but from his general comments about trying insanity cases it is easy to reconstruct the factors he weighed. First, he was concerned that the elaborate biochemical evidence Altschule had gathered over almost two years would be too complex for a lay jury to assimilate in a matter of just a few days. Moreover, he knew that under Massachusetts procedural rules he would have no chance to question prospective jurors as to their attitudes about insanity. Finally, Roseman anticipated that in the absence of a jury, a judge was likely to be more flexible, particularly in admitting the novel evidence on which the defense was relying.

All of these considerations were apparent almost from the outset, yet in his legal research Roseman devoted special attention to jury instructions. The defense did not decide to waive the jury until just before the case was called—and after it was announced that Thomas Dwyer would hear it. Roseman had never tried a case before Dwyer (whereas O'Boy had), but he knew of him as a brilliant trial lawyer and a scrupulously fair judge. According to O'Boy, "Dwyer runs a tight ship, but he is easy to try in front of—provided you know what you are doing." In capital cases and in federal court, jury waiver requires the prosecution's assent, but here the choice was solely the defendant's. Dwyer's reputation for intelligence and fairness may have tipped the balance.

During the first day and a half of trial, when Frank O'Boy presented the Commonwealth's case against Decker, little came out to shake Judge Dwyer's initial skepticism about the defendant's irresponsibility claim. On Monday, Gail Sussman told the court how Decker had suddenly and savagely attacked her and her friend Deborah Sharp, beaten them into semiconsciousness, and left them with fractured skulls by the roadside. In his cross-examination, David Roseman made no attempt to challenge her testimony. Instead, he made her confirm some of its most shocking details. Roseman sensed that Dwyer did regard the facts as peculiar—the seemingly unprovoked attack, and the defendant's equally sudden shift from rage to remorse—but clearly these circumstances alone were not enough to prove insanity. Now that the prosecution had established the facts, it was up to the defense to present testimony that would somehow explain them.

With court permission, Roseman could have made his opening right after the prosecutor completed his on Monday morning, but because he had already outlined his approach to the judge informally, the lawyer elected to wait until O'Boy had presented the prosecution's case. Nothing that a lawyer says by way of opening is accepted as formal evidence—all contentions have to be documented through subsequent testimony—but a successful opening can set the tone of an entire trial. It is intended to give the fact finder, in this case the judge, a preview of the evidence, so that he will have a basis for comprehending and evaluating it as it is presented. Roseman likens the function of an opening to "the reading of a libretto setting forth the characters and the story before one hears the opera."

The opening is one phase of the trial over which a lawyer has rather precise control. There are no surprise statements by witnesses and no interruptions from counsel for the other side. Roseman wanted to use the opportunity to impress on the judge that this was an unusual case, one built on hard laboratory data, not on ambiguous and possibly self-serving psychiatric interviews with the accused. During the year and a half he had spent preparing the defense, Roseman had sometimes seen himself as a playwright polishing his script, rehearsing his lines, imagining how his production would look and sound to its audience of one. On Tuesday morning he was still recovering from the flu, but he was not daunted. The show must go on. He rose.

"Your Honor," Roseman began, "I think I perhaps should first say formally that the defense of the defendant to these charges is that at the time of the alleged conduct on July 17, 1974, the defendant was criminally irresponsible within the meaning of the American Law Institute rule—which I understand is that a person is not responsible for criminal conduct if at the time of such conduct, as a result of a mental disease or a mental defect, he lacked substantial capacity either to conform his conduct to the requirements of law, or appreciate the criminality or the wrongfulness of his conduct—"

"In which tests, or both?" interrupted Judge Dwyer.

"On both, Your Honor."

Roseman wanted to keep all options open, but by transposing the ALI standard, putting incapacity to conform to the law ahead of inability to understand it, the lawyer had signaled that he thought the former would be easier to prove. Roseman's introduction also indicated that he would walk a thin line. He persisted in referring to the "alleged" crime, refusing to concede his client's actions; yet, as indicated in his cross-examination of Sussman, he was prepared to argue the case on the assumption that the attacks had taken place just as the prosecution claimed.

Roseman next summarized, in the most favorable light, what his witnesses and evidence were intended to show. He gave a brief description of Charles's background: he was twenty-two, with a wife and child, and employed at the time of the arrest; he lived near his parents; his father was a scientist with the Navy. The lawyer described his chief witness, Dr. Mark Altschule, as a specialist in "the field of behavior caused by physiological or by chemical disorders; to put it another way, concerned with the nonmental causes of mental and emotional disturbances, the biochemistry of mental disease." Altschule, he explained, would testify that the defendant "suffered from a dysfunction or lesion in the limbic system of his brain" that rendered him irresponsible under the ALI test.

The lawyer turned toward an easel set up before the bench, on which was mounted a large chart. The chart displayed two contrasting figures. "If Your Honor will just look at that chart we have on the board, you will see the large white area with the canals. That area—"

"Take a pointer and point it out to me," Dwyer interjected. "I'm starting with a broad foundation of ignorance."

Roseman picked up the pointer and assumed the posture of a lecturer. He was no biochemist, but, tutored by Mark Altschule and Nicholas Decker, he had mastered everything he needed to know about the science of this case. Now it was time to pass the lessons on to Judge Dwyer. Roseman pointed to the lower of the two figures, a large outline of the human brain. The white area, he explained, was the cortex, where the intellectual functions of the brain are located. The ability to rationalize, evaluate, and form ideas — the functions that distinguish man from the lower animals — are cortical. This first figure was predominantly white, for the human brain is mostly cortex. Tucked underneath the cortex was a much smaller gray area representing the heart-shaped limbic system — the part of the defendant's brain Dr. Altschule had found to be malfunctioning.

As in other animals, Roseman continued, the limbic system in man reacts to external stimuli, and initiates such responses as fright, aggression, assaultive behavior, and flight. In the healthy human brain, however, the limbic system is subservient to the highly developed cortical system. For example, the lawyer noted, the limbic system may react to a shadow with "immediate stark fear," but then "the cortical system will evaluate that impulse and tell you that you are in your house and merely seeing your own shadow, and the body will relax." By contrast, he went on, when the connections between the limbic system and the cortex are disturbed or when the limbus itself is dysfunctional, this control breaks down, and the individual may display aberrant behavior, including irrational violence. This is the result of the primitive limbic brain acting alone, ungoverned.

Roseman moved his pointer from the silhouette of the human brain to a second, contrasting diagram labeled "crocodile." Here, too, was a brain, but this one was much smaller and almost all gray limbic system, with only a narrow white strip of cortex. Roseman was arguing that the same limbic system that dominates the crocodile's brain lives within us all.

*

The crocodile is noted among herpetologists for its intelligence and curiosity. It can be tamed, learn to recognize its keepers, accept petting, and even beg for food. The maternal instinct of the female crocodile is stronger than that of any other cold-blooded animal. These are not the qualities upon which the crocodile's reputation rests, however.

There are some twenty species in the order *Crocodylia,* including, in addition to various types of crocodiles, the alligators, the caimans, and the fish-eating gharials with their slender snouts. All are aquatic, but most are also at home on dry land, where, running on extended legs, they are capable of short bursts of astonishing speed. The largest specimens today are not more than twenty to twenty-five feet long, but early tales of monsters of over thirty feet are plausible, since modern firearms and the commercial demand for hides have probably eliminated the oldest individuals. With no enemies save man, crocodiles have long natural lifespans—a half-century or more—and they continue to grow throughout their lives.

Only two species, one in Africa and one in Asia, are confirmed man-eaters. (The sole known killing by an American alligator occurred when a careless hunter approached an insufficiently dead trophy.) The Nile crocodile terrorizes certain riverside villages, while unaccountably showing fear of man in nearby areas. In some herds, particular creatures are identified as habitual killers. The Nile species is the subject of the familiar legends of the crocodile. Most experts, however, contend that the estuarine crocodile, a salt-water species of coastal South Asia, the Malay Archipelago, and the Pacific as far as Fiji, is even more dangerous. A well-attested instance of its viciousness occurred on February 19, 1945, on Ramree Island on the Burmese side of the Bay of Bengal. British troops, cleaning out pockets of Japanese resistance, had trapped a thousand enemy soldiers in a seacoast swamp. As night fell and the crocodiles moved in, the British heard screams of horror and pain. No one can tell how many of the Japanese were killed by the crocodiles, how many stumbled into the water in panic, and how many were ordinary casualties of war, but next morning only twenty men surrendered.

Crocodiles do, in fact, shed tears, but the best authorities agree that despite possessing the most highly developed brains of any reptile, they are not capable of hypocrisy as we know it.

Some believe that their unfavorable image in this regard derives from their ever-present "grin"; others attribute it to their eerie sobbing howl. A more likely source is the crocodilian habit of lying placidly near game trails or floating still as a log at water's edge, then suddenly lunging at their prey, swiping it into the water to be drowned or torn limb from limb by powerful jaws studded with more than a hundred continually growing teeth. Such attacks are triggered by the reptile's limbic system.

*

As an image of unrestrained viciousness, Roseman could hardly have chosen better than the crocodile. (He had copied his chart from Mark and Ervin's *Violence and the Brain*.) Certainly the display would have had less impact if the human brain had been contrasted with that of, say, a turtle. The lawyer started to describe in greater detail the behavioral implications of limbic dysfunction, but Judge Dwyer cut him off, saying "This is more of an argument than an opening." Roseman had wanted to go as far as he could without testing his audience's indulgence; he cut short his overture and introduced the star of his drama.

The entire defense rested on the testimony of Dr. Mark Altschule. This was just as Roseman wanted it. At first he had considered supplementing the physician's testimony with psychiatric evidence, and Charles had been examined by a specialist who was ready to swear that the young man was criminally irresponsible. Yet Roseman ultimately decided against using a second witness. "It's not a game of numbers," he explains. "It's a game of credibility — credibility in the sense of having a design that makes sense, having follow-through, having internal consistency in all aspects of that opinion."

Even though the psychiatrist who had examined Charles had reached the same conclusion, the fact that he came to it by quite different procedures necessarily would have weakened the impact of Altschule's presentation. The recent *Ricard* decision had taught Roseman that even uncontroverted psychiatric evidence may not be enough to establish insanity. In *Ricard* and other court opinions there seemed to be an underlying skepticism of psychiatric evidence of insanity, which usually rests on interviews with the defendant himself. It was essential, Roseman concluded, that his case be clearly distinguishable from the rest. "I divided in my own mind hard data—numbers, firm test procedures—from interpretation. And I wanted interpretation to be kept to a minimum."

Roseman also was prepared to bank on Altschule because he was the defendant's physician, not simply an expert retained to testify in court. (Roseman recalls a former federal-court judge privately complaining that experts in trials are "a bunch of God-damned paid liars.") Dr. Altschule had seen Charles Decker regularly over the previous two years and had also examined him as a teen-ager. "Altschule was very important to me," says Roseman, "because not only did he have enormous credentials, he was the treating physician. After all, he was testifying about his patient, and he was doing so to convince the court that his patient was ill. The issue of guilt or nonguilt in a criminal proceeding was not really relevant to the professional diagnosis."

Consistency was the principal reason for relying on Altschule alone, but there was another consideration. If Roseman called the psychiatrist to testify, then in cross-examination O'Boy would have a better opportunity to delve into the defendant's personal history. There were matters in Charles Decker's past— notably his earlier violent episodes—that Roseman did not want brought out.

On the other hand, a psychiatrist would have qualified automatically as an expert witness in the field of mental health, while Altschule's status in this regard was open to challenge. Only designated expert witnesses are allowed to go beyond statements of fact and offer opinions on technical matters. Recognized fields of expertise range from ballistics to appraisal to graphology. Qualification as an expert depends on standards of training, experience, and certification. Because Altschule was not board-certified in either psychiatry or neurology, Roseman would have to persuade the court, against O'Boy's certain opposition, to accept him as an expert on the particular type of disorder at issue in the case. The defense lawyer knew it was a gamble, but on the basis of his research and his instincts, he thought the risk was not great. Yet if he lost this skirmish, his entire trial strategy would collapse, and his only recourse would be appeal.

Altschule was called forward to testify, not at first about his patient but to establish his own qualifications as an expert. Unlike Gail Sussman the day before, he stood erect on the witness stand, despite his years. He took a moment to adjust his hearing aid, and then, under Roseman's examination, he met the issue of his expertise head-on. "I am not a psychiatrist," he testified. "However, my special interest is the physiology-biochemistry of strange reactions of all types, physical and mental. I have published extensively on those subjects." Roseman had him explain just how extensively he had published — ten or twelve books, hundreds of articles — and went on to elicit all the aspects of the physician's background that made him a qualified witness: his decades of practice at McLean and elsewhere; his medical teaching at Harvard, Yale, Tufts, Boston University, and other universities; his consulting position with the Office of Naval Research; his list of professional affiliations and membership on editorial boards.

As the litany went on, the judge tried to cut it short by suggesting that the prosecution might be willing to accept Altschule's expertise without challenge: "Let me see if the Commonwealth has objection to qualifying the doctor in the area outlined by the attorney in his opening."

"I do, Your Honor," O'Boy responded.

Lawyers do not lightly disregard suggestions from the bench. Surely O'Boy could read Dwyer's remark as an indication that the judge had already heard enough to regard Altschule as an expert, and that any further questioning would be a waste of the court's time. Nonetheless O'Boy persisted. Even if he did not prevail, he could hope to use the process to underscore the limits of the witness's expertise.

Roseman continued his questioning, turning at once to the specific point at issue, Altschule's knowledge of mental health. The physician testified that he had just published a book on the history of psychiatry, which he had been asked to write—this over O'Boy's objection—because he was not committed to any one school of psychiatry. He also noted that he had published two articles on Korsakoff's syndrome, with the neurologist Maurice Victor, in 1957. (Victor, now at Case Western Reserve University, is regarded as the leading authority on this disease.) Roseman then closed by trying to introduce Altschule's long association with Charles Decker as part of his qualifications, but O'Boy objected on the grounds that this constituted discussion of the specific case.

Next it was the prosecutor's turn to challenge the physician's status as an expert through cross-examination. Like many others before and since, O'Boy quickly learned that bandying words with Mark Altschule can be frustrating.

"Doctor," he began, "have you ever testified before in any court of the Commonwealth or any other jurisdiction—"

"I testified in this room," Altschule shot back.

"I didn't complete my question; let me, if you would—on the question of sanity of a patient of yours?"

"No, not in this jurisdiction," the physician admitted. "I did in Vermont."

"You never testified in the Commonwealth of Massachusetts?"

"No."

"Have you ever testified in any other jurisdiction," O'Boy pursued, "on a question of the sanity of a defendant in a criminal case?"

Roseman objected to this question, but Dwyer overruled the objection. Though Altschule may merely have been sparring, he made the right response: "I find difficulty in understanding what you mean by that, because the patients with respect to whom I testified were patients in a mental hospital."

Roseman's objection had been to O'Boy's use of the word *sanity*. The legal rule upon which the defense relied did not speak of sanity, but of the defendant's "responsibility" for his actions at the moment of his act. This distinction was particularly important in the Decker case, because Roseman's argument was that Charles was not insane in the familiar sense of the word. Moreover, it was important, specifically, in establishing Altschule's qualifications as an expert witness: the court might accept an internist as an expert on the transitory psychic effects of physical illness, but regard full-fledged insanity as the province of psychiatry. Finally, a favorable disposition of the case depended on the judge's understanding that Charles Decker's problem could best be dealt with through medical treatment, not institutionalization. Altschule's answer went to the heart of the distinction Roseman wanted made. Dwyer did not change his ruling, but he acknowledged the point.

O'Boy returned to his struggle with the witness. "And would you agree with me, Doctor, that the determination of sanity or insanity as it relates to criminal responsibility is a field which is occupied by psychiatrists?"

"It is occupied by psychiatrists, I agree," the physician responded sarcastically.

"Would you feel that a psychiatrist would be the most qualified person to express an opinion on the sanity or insanity as it relates to the patient's criminal responsibility?"

"The most qualified?" asked Altschule with emphasis.

"Yes."

"Not necessarily."

O'Boy proceeded to bring out the fact that Altschule had received no special training in psychiatry. Then he turned to the witness's duties at McLean, stressing (over Altschule's corrections of his terminology) that the physician had not been part of the psychiatric unit. "And how many departments are there at McLean?" O'Boy asked.

"I would say that apart from my special department, there was only one other," explained Altschule. "That consisted of all the rest of the staff."

O'Boy continued to volley with Altschule, winning some points, losing others. Altschule was persuasive in declaring that mental abnormalities are not solely the province of psychiatry, but sometimes his argumentative style led him into overstatements. Toward the end of the cross-examination, for example, he started to say that physical injuries to the brain do not necessarily fall within the fields of neurology and neurosurgery, but was interrupted by Judge Dwyer, who was openly skeptical of Altschule's position. "Where else would that go? What other discipline would that go to?" the judge asked. Perhaps Altschule sensed that he had been too contentious, at least in this unfamiliar setting. After the judge's reaction, the physician's answers were more restrained.

O'Boy closed his questioning and renewed his objection to qualifying Altschule as an expert, but Judge Dwyer, having heard both sides, ruled that the physician could testify.

*

This victory, though not unexpected, was crucial. The court had granted the defense the opportunity to make its case. Roseman had devoted more than a year, and five hundred billable hours, to preparation for this moment. Altschule had spent a professional lifetime fashioning his contribution. Together they would have a single day to educate the judge.

They had to work, moreover, under significant constraints. Roseman felt that Altschule had acquitted himself well so far, and had made a favorable impression on Judge Dwyer. Yet he had to be concerned about the physician's propensity for saying what he pleased, for there were certain points he must not bring up in his testimony. Some of these were matters that might seem to help the case, or even, in Altschule's mind, be integral to it. The defense had to tread a number of very fine lines.

Roseman's basic task was to present testimony that would persuade the judge, first, that Charles Decker suffered from a physiological defect; and second, that under the ALI/*McHoul* test, that defect resulted in an incapacity either to appreciate the criminality of his actions or to conform them to the law. To do this, he and Altschule had to advance evidence that depended directly on Charles's drinking. At the same time, Roseman had to make it clear, both in the questions he posed and in the answers he sought, that Charles's behavior did not fall under the Massachusetts rule relating to voluntary consumption of alcohol. For the same reason, he had to suppress the details of his client's prior history of violence that could have alerted him to his condition, while simultaneously using this record of inappropriate behavior to justify the diagnosis of limbic dysfunction. He likewise had to make sure that Charles's own account of provocation did not emerge to cast doubt on the perfect irrationality of the crime. Finally, he knew that O'Boy would challenge Altschule's testimony both directly and by presenting his own expert in rebuttal. Roseman hoped he could keep his feisty witness under tight rein.

Having established the physician's general expertise in the qualification process, Roseman opened his direct examination by presenting him as an authority in the specific case of Charles Decker. He brought out Altschule's seven-year relationship with Charles, his association with Nicholas Decker, and his long involvement in the present case. The physician testified that he had heard Gail Sussman's eyewitness account of the assault at the probable-cause hearing less than a month after the event, and once again in court the previous day. These preliminary points, of course, provided the foundation for Altschule's diagnosis of Charles's condition. Just as important, they established that the witness for the defense would speak from firsthand knowledge. The prosecution's expert, whatever his other qualifications, had neither examined Charles nor heard the girl's testimony (though he would have seen a transcript).

In some European legal systems, a witness simply takes the stand and delivers a monologue relating everything he knows about the case, but in American courts testimony must be developed through a structured dialogue between the witness and the lawyer interrogating him. Moreover, in direct examination the lawyer is not allowed to ask leading questions. This prohibition is aimed at preventing the lawyer from putting words in the witness's mouth; it also gives the attorney for the other side a chance to object before the witness can testify about impermissible subjects.

Throughout his appearance, Altschule bridled at the rigid formality of the examination, impatient with narrow questions that did not allow him to give a full explanation of his methods and findings. Still, under Roseman's guidance he was able to describe the sequence of his work: first the inconclusive alcohol-tolerance test, then the discovery of Charles's case of Korsakoff's syndrome. The physician went on to outline the psychological manifestations of Korsakoff's syndrome, and its physical appearance, a spotty lesion in the limbic area. The judge, apparently intrigued by the idea of solid physical evidence, asked, "Can you see it?" Altschule assured him that you could, under a microscope.

Roseman hastened to prevent a misunderstanding. "Can you see it in a person who is alive?" he asked.

"We are not allowed to do that kind of thing," Altschule replied.

"Now," continued Roseman, "does a limbic lesion have any manifestations as far as behavior is concerned?"

"Well," replied Altschule, "since it governs the generation and expression of emotion, that is what it does. As a rule, in an animal that is all there is. In the case of human beings, the function of the limbic system is modulated, regulated by the cortex."

"What is the cortex?" pursued Roseman.

"The cortex is the outer layer and is the part of the brain that is supposed to separate men from beasts."

"In what respect?"

"In the sense that it is responsible for reasoning, for abstract interpretation, and also for controlling the animal emotion generated in the limbic system."

"Assume one were to have a dysfunction in the limbic system as you have described," said the lawyer. "What if any relation would that have to behavior?"

"A limbic lesion is manifested by a particular kind of attack," explained the physician. "It would be manifested by unpremeditated, unprovoked, unpredictable sudden onset of manifestations during which the patient behaves irrationally, at the end of which, when it is over, he behaves perfectly normally. During the attack, or, put it this way, after the attack, his memory of the events will be fragmentary and often inaccurate — that is to say, not only does he not remember things that happened, but he may remember things that didn't happen. That is the nature of a limbic attack, which was brilliantly described by Dr. Mark in his book."

The stage was set for the defense's *pièce de résistance.* Korsakoff's syndrome was an indication of physical brain damage, but diagnosis of the condition itself depended on mere verbal and behavioral evidence — a point the judge had raised on his own. In addition, because Korsakoff's syndrome was generally linked with alcoholism, mention of its presence would invite a riposte by the prosecution on the voluntary-drinking issue. The results of the later blood tests, however, were firm laboratory evidence of the defendant's physical abnormality; and these results were evidence that apparently called into question a simple attribution of Charles's violence to his drinking. Roseman could not conceal the gaps and uncertainties in his case, but he could hope that the verifiable nature of the cause he adduced would make up for the fact that its effect, though plausible, was entirely speculative.

With Dwyer and O'Boy helping to keep Altschule on a factual, chronological course, Roseman led his witness through a description of his series of tests. The early electroencephalograms, which detected no unusual cortical discharges, came first. Then the physician returned to his blood tests. Roseman had him explain the two methods of measuring blood alcohol — gas chromatography and enzyme analysis — and then called him down from the stand to where two charts stood on easels facing the bench. One showed the results of the assays of May 21 and May 22 in graph form. The gas-chromatograph registers of blood alcohol were represented by squares connected by dotted lines; circles linked by solid lines showed the enzyme-method results for the same blood samples. On the chart, the broken and solid lines diverged markedly, with the enzyme-method figures consistently higher.

After Altschule had expanded on the graph headings and given a brief summary of his experimental procedure, Roseman asked him what the diverging lines meant. The physician replied that the gas-chromatograph measurement was very accurate, while the enzyme reading necessarily included "something else plus the alcohol, something resembling alcohol but not alcohol."

"What did that lead you to conclude?" the lawyer asked.

"Well," Altschule responded, "it led me to conclude that when he was given alcohol he developed something in his blood that was similar to alcohol but was not alcohol. All we can say is it has not been identified yet."

"Unidentified substance?"

"Yes. Since it resembled alcohol in its reactions with enzymes, I would conclude that it was a toxic substance."

"When you say *toxic,* what do you mean by *toxic?*" asked Roseman.

"Poisonous," replied the physician.

"Does that have any relation to the lesion that you described?"

"I believe it does. Since it's unidentified I can't be sure."

"Do you have a medical opinion as to a reasonable medical certainty?"

Here the prosecutor objected, but futilely.

"My opinion," said Altschule, "is that when he drinks, something is generated in his blood which in my opinion is damaging to his brain."

"And in what respect is it damaging to his brain?" asked Roseman.

"I would conclude that since the substance resembled alcohol but is not quite alcohol that the injury done to the brain would be similar to that of alcohol." This was a key speculative link in Altschule's theory.

Roseman pressed on. "What injury, if any, does alcohol do to the brain?"

"It produces limbic damage," the witness replied.

*

Proof of Charles Decker's metabolic dysfunction was now before the court, together with his physician's theory of its relationship to the crime. The defense attorney's next task was to distinguish the beer the young man had drunk on the evening of July 17—indeed, all the alcohol he had drunk voluntarily over the years—from the mysterious alcohol-like substance in his blood. Roseman asked Altschule to turn to the second chart, which presented, again in graph form, the findings of July 29 and July 30. "What is that test?" he asked.

Indicating the single curve (in this case, the assay had been by enzyme alone), Altschule noted two anomalies. "We found that this unknown substance, unidentified substance, was increasing even after the alcohol stopped," he said, pointing to a continuing rise beyond the label indicating when alcohol was administered, "and that instead of coming down within six or eight hours, which alcohol would, it stayed in the blood for twenty-six hours or longer."

The lawyer understood exactly what the chart showed, of course, but he feigned ignorance to reinforce the point. "What was increasing even after the alcohol stopped?" he asked.

"This unidentified substance," Altschule explained, ostensibly to Roseman.

His examiner continued to play dumb. "I don't quite follow what you mean."

"We stopped giving alcohol and turned off at the end of one hour," said the physician, "and the amount of this unidentified substance, instead of staying the same at the end of one hour, it continued to increase..." Then he added, as if as an after-thought, the more important point. "Also, I should like to point out here"—he indicated the first reading on the chart—"that before he got any alcohol he already had almost eighty milligrams per cent [per cubic centimeter] in his blood of this unknown substance. Before he even got the alcohol it was up to there. We had seen that on other tests too; even in the absence of alcohol the substance would appear in this man."

"When you say 'before he got alcohol,'" Roseman said ingenuously, "you mean alcohol that day?..."

"This might have been three weeks."

"I don't quite understand," said the lawyer, wanting to make sure the court did.

Altschule elaborated: At the time of the reading, which showed the presence of an alcohol-like substance in his blood, Charles Decker had not taken a drink in three weeks. Judge Dwyer appeared skeptical of this startling piece of testimony. "Was he supervised all during the time?" he asked. Yes, replied Altschule, but at his home, not in confinement. "He wasn't in any clinic?" Dwyer asked. Although Roseman disagrees, the judge apparently was taking this finding with a grain of salt.

This was a point of some danger for the defense, and not merely because the credibility of the latent-substance finding was in question. If Altschule overstated his case on this matter, he risked his personal credibility in the judge's eyes. His unorthodox and underfinanced tests also might appear to be unreliable "homemade experiments." Had Dwyer persisted in the questioning, or had O'Boy picked up the thread, the involvement of Nicholas Decker might have tumbled out and compromised the tenability of the entire defense. Roseman and Altschule proceeded to shore up the credibility of their conclusion by demonstrating that within the test period, when Charles was certainly under direct observation, the concentration of the substance in his blood had continued to fluctuate in an erratic and unexpected manner. The unidentified "poison," their figures implied, was not present as a direct, predictable result of the young man's drinking.

Nevertheless, Roseman's final piece of new evidence actually raised again the possibility of a connection between Charles's drinking and his mental state. Roseman had Altschule describe his second test for Korsakoff's syndrome, in May, which had revealed no deficit in mental function. This indicated that the limbic lesion had undergone "marked healing"; and the physician's opinion was that "it healed because he never took another drink again." Altschule cited his own study, published nearly two decades earlier, which indicated that such recovery was possible.

Roseman had largely completed his examination, but Dwyer, free of the inhibition of a jury, jumped in with questions of his own. He turned to the witness and said, "You work deductively then; don't you?" Altschule assented. "You put a lot of the weight of your opinion on the incident itself and state it is symptomatic of this syndrome, then he has the syndrome because you find an unidentified substance in his blood which has a toxic reaction like alcohol, and you therefore put those factors together and say that he was not criminally responsible?"

Altschule replied that he would have placed his emphasis a bit differently, but that the judge was correct, he did work deductively. "We have to. We can't take the man apart." The physician, who had sometimes been sarcastic with O'Boy and balky with Roseman, seemed more at ease with his new inquisitor—perhaps less out of deference than out of respect. "That judge amazed me," he recalled later. "I have a great deal of admiration for the way he handled that situation that was totally new to him, and involved data that he had difficulty in grasping...He was highly intelligent—not only skillful in the law, but highly intelligent."

Dwyer wanted to be very sure he understood Altschule's position. What, he wanted to know, would the physician's conclusion have been if he had had only the test results, without any knowledge of an assault? Would he have made the same diagnosis? "Yes," replied the witness, "if he had inappropriate behavior of any kind."

"No," insisted Dwyer. "No assault. His father brings him in your office and says, 'I want him checked up,' and you do all these tests. And you have all these findings identical to your testimony here today, no nonconformist behavior."

"Then he does not have the syndrome," returned Altschule. "You have to have evidence of damage by the substance before you conclude there is damage. We know that people have different tolerances. For example, not everybody, to change the subject a bit if I may, not everybody who drinks heavily ends up with Korsakoff's syndrome. Not everybody who drinks heavily ends up with liver disease or heart disease. There is an enormous range of tolerance between people, and so if we took five hundred people after a big banquet and measured their blood alcohol, you might find them all the same and only a small number may have some syndrome as a result of it."

For the moment, the judge had taken over Roseman's witness; but Roseman himself could not have elicited a better answer. The time was five minutes past one, the usual lunch hour. It had been a grueling morning, and O'Boy's cross-examination and a second round of medical evidence—from the prosecution's expert—were still to come. Dwyer hoped that Roseman's direct examination was finished, but the defense lawyer asked for ten minutes more. The judge, taking into account the complexity of the defense's case and the feistiness of the witness, doubted this estimate and called for a break. When the court reconvened after lunch, however, Roseman had only one basic question—though a large one—for Altschule. He wanted the physician to draw together all the threads of testimony that had been developed that morning.

To set the stage, he had Altschule reconfirm his conclusion that on the evening of July 17, 1974, Charles Decker was not responsible for his actions according to the ALI/*McHoul* guidelines. Then, to allow his witness to summarize, he asked again, "What is the basis for that opinion?"

Altschule was thoroughly prepared with his answer. "The basis for that opinion is the fact that I made a diagnosis of a limbic lesion in him. That diagnosis is based upon several items. One is the nature of the attack, which was out of the clear sky, unpremeditated, violent, irrational. And when it terminated it was followed immediately by normal, moral behavior, and he had a fragmented memory of it."

Underscoring his point, Altschule said, "The nature of the attack is one thing." Then he continued, "The second is that when I did my test on him in March for memory and ability to incorporate the new, recently acquired information, I found him abnormal in March. And the third thing is the finding in his blood plus what he drank and long after he drank, of a substance resembling alcohol that I believe to be toxic. Does that answer the question?"

"It does," said Roseman. "I have no further questions."

\*

Jonathan Otis Cole, M.D., the prosecution expert in rebuttal, was champing at the bit, so eager was he to give his testimony. "The high point of that trial," remarked Altschule, "was his demand that he be called at two o'clock and no later—he said his wife would kill him if he got home late. And the D.A. said, 'Don't worry, Doc, we'll get her a good lawyer.'"

O'Boy had good reason to want to defuse the tension caused by his witness's impatience. Altschule, in the end, had proved a strong witness on direct questioning, and obviously had established rapport with the judge. His testimony would be hard enough to counter from an even start. Now O'Boy's own expert was making demands of the court, and courts are notoriously peevish about being hurried.

Cole's busy schedule had already necessitated a departure from normal trial procedure in that he was appearing as a rebuttal witness before the opposition's expert had been cross-examined. Each lawyer felt that this change in sequence helped his case. O'Boy was glad to have Cole take the stand right after Altschule left it, so that he could weigh in with an authoritative debunking of the physician's theories. Roseman, in turn, felt that the shift gave him a double advantage. Altschule would now have a chance to hear his critic, and then respond to him in cross-examination. Moreover, Altschule, not Cole, would have the last word before the judge.

Following the same procedure Roseman had used in the morning, the assistant district attorney qualified his expert by having him recite his credentials. They were impressive. Cole was not yet fifty, but he had been involved in psychiatry for almost thirty years, having received his M.D. from Cornell at twenty-one. He had served as director of the psychopharmacology research program at the National Institute of Mental Health; superintendent of Boston State Hospital and professor of psychiatry at Tufts University; chairman of the department of psychiatry at Temple University, in Philadelphia; and, for the past two years, head of the psychiatric pharmacology program at McLean, with an appointment at Harvard Medical School. (Although Cole had known Altschule since his student days, he had not joined the McLean staff until after the older man's retirement from full-time work there.)

In planning his response to Roseman and Altschule's argument of physical brain dysfunction, O'Boy had worried about "playing in the other guy's ballpark." With Jonathan Cole as the state witness, he had at least drafted an all-star. The psychopharmacologist was internationally recognized as a leading expert on the physical components of mental illness. Nor was there any question about his formal qualifications. He had received regular training in psychiatry and belonged to all the appropriate professional societies. He had also published more than a hundred articles in the field. Dwyer accepted him as an expert witness without hesitation, and without objection from the defense.

On the stand, too, Cole was impressive, as he redefined the concepts at issue—Korsakoff's syndrome, limbic lesion, and the rest—in his own clear, concise terms. Then, under O'Boy's guidance, he began to attack Altschule's methods and conclusions. He spoke with perfect assurance. Yes, he said, there were objective tests for limbic lesions: EEGs with nasopharyngeal leads were valuable, and CAT-scans gave "a lovely picture." What about the memory and retained-information test? "I have great difficulty in making a specific diagnosis of limbic-lobe damage on the basis of any evidence other than CAT-scan and positive brain-wave testing," Cole replied.

He had not examined Charles Decker, Cole admitted, but he had read records of his examinations at Bridgewater and Shattuck, as well as the transcript of Gail Sussman's testimony. He had also heard Mark Altschule's evidence that morning. O'Boy asked whether based on all that information, he had an opinion as to whether the defendant had had a limbic-lobe lesion. "I do not believe he did," answered Cole.

David Roseman responded with a torrent of objections. Cole had just denied the contention that was the linchpin of his defense case, but Roseman was concerned not just with the psychiatrist's conclusion but also with the evidence he had used to arrive at it. The lawyer felt that at all costs he had to keep out of the record those Bridgewater reports containing both Charles's own account of the assault and references to his prior history of violence. Citing both the state statute excluding such records and the Fifth Amendment *Miranda* rule, he insisted that O'Boy rephrase each of his questions to his witness so as to eliminate consideration of the Bridgewater material explicitly.

Judge Dwyer was at first sympathetic to the defense lawyer, but he became increasingly annoyed at what he obviously regarded as Roseman's nit-picking. When Dwyer dismissed Roseman's final, thoroughly trivial objection and invited Cole to repeat his answer to the previous question, however, the defense seemed to reap an unexpected dividend from the diversion. This time, the psychiatrist's assessment of Charles Decker's condition was more equivocal: "Insofar as one can have an affirmative opinion when you weren't there at the time and have not examined the individual in question, I do not believe there is any definite evidence of limbic-orb disorder."

But Cole regained his assurance as O'Boy proceeded to the ALI/*McHoul* standard. Could Charles Decker "appreciate the wrongfulness or criminality of his act"? O'Boy asked.

"To the same extent as most intoxicated individuals have when engaged in aggressive behavior," Cole answered. "Intoxicated with alcohol, one engages in aggressive behavior."

Could he conform his conduct to the law? "He was able to the same extent that inebriated individuals can in fact do that," Cole said. What if, hypothetically, he did have limbic damage? Would that affect his ability to appreciate the criminality of his actions, or control them? "I do not believe that it differs substantially than that possessed by any other intoxicated individual," concluded the witness.

Cole was saying that at the time of the assault, Charles Decker had been drunk. In Cole's view, he had not been suffering from limbic-lobe damage, and even if he had, it would not explain or excuse his aggressive behavior. This was a blow straight at the heart of the defense's case, but it was a weak blow. Cole was contradicting Altschule's diagnosis, yet Altschule was an experienced physician with special qualifications in the field, who had examined and tested Charles Decker.

O'Boy concluded by raising the question of voluntary drinking. Was there, he asked, a condition known as pathological intoxication? Yes, replied the witness, that term referred to highly abnormal or violent behavior occurring when the aggressor was drunk. Did Cole have an opinion as to whether Charles's drinking was voluntary? Yes, the defendant "appeared to be acting under his own volition in picking up the girls and going to his house and getting more beer and marijuana."

It was Roseman's turn to cross-examine the opposing expert witness. In this role the lawyer was free to ask leading, even argumentative questions. Cole's evidence had been damaging to his case, but it could have been worse. The psychiatrist's assured, positive answers had been too good to be true—too pat, too general, and insufficiently responsive to the particular facts at hand.

Roseman sensed that if he could expose Cole's ignorance of specific aspects of the case, he could cripple the credibility of the prosecution witness's facile generalizations. At the same time, any admission favorable to the defense that he could coax from the psychiatrist would carry special weight.

The defense attorney began his cross-examination by establishing that Cole knew Altschule, knew of his fine reputation in the medical community, and regarded him as "a careful and thorough doctor." Even among medical colleagues who are at each other's throats in private, such commendations are virtually inevitable. Then he went on to examine the psychiatrist's own knowledge of the case. He had not examined Charles Decker?

"Correct," conceded Cole.

"As a matter of fact, you never even saw him until you walked into the courtroom today?"

"Quite correct."

"You never heard the testimony of Miss Sussman at any time; did you?"

"No, I did not."

"All you were given were statements which the prosecutor had provided you?"

"Yes, that's true."

"As a matter of fact," insisted Roseman, "you don't know

whether Mr. Decker on July 17, 1974, was inebriated or drunk at any time?"

"Only by what I have read," the witness responded.

Roseman pounced. "Were you told that Miss Sussman yesterday stated on three occasions that to her Mr. Decker did not appear to be drunk?"

"No," admitted Cole. He had dismissed the defendant's condition as mere intoxication, without realizing that the victim's own testimony—the only admissible source of evidence about the circumstances of the crime—cast doubt on his conclusion.

Roseman was homing in on the greatest weakness of Cole's testimony, the psychiatrist's failure to acknowledge the apparent anomalies of Charles's case. "If he were not drunk would that change your opinion in any respect?" the lawyer asked.

"That's a hard question," Cole responded. "I would say if he had been drinking alcohol and behaved in this manner I would infer that he was drunk. If he was not drunk, no. If he had shown similar behavior on other times when not drinking alcohol, I would look more deeply for a neurological diagnosis."

"And, of course," Roseman noted, "you have never made any attempt to make any kind of neurological diagnosis?" Of course, Cole had not.

The lawyer then went on to the matter of Altschule's procedures and results. Isn't it a fact, he asked, that the ultimate test for a limbic lesion is through autopsy? Cole agreed it was.

"Now you, of course, were not present when Dr. Altschule ran these alcohol-tolerance tests?" Roseman queried.

"That's true, true."

"And you have not seen his data?"

"No," the psychiatrist admitted.

Cole conceded that there were, according to the assay results, unknown alcohol-like substances in Charles Decker's blood. He acknowledged that Korsakoff's syndrome could be caused by substances other than alcohol itself, and did occur in nonalcoholics. Its appearance depended on "body chemistry," or "unknown factors."

Roseman could hardly have hoped for a clearer echo of Altschule's "unknown substance." He closed as he had begun, with a confirmation of his own witness's credentials.

O'Boy took up his redirect examination at that point. If a lawyer is, as Roseman suggests, something of a playwright and director, then legal productions can become increasingly extemporaneous. In trying to patch the holes in his witness's testimony exposed by cross-examination, the prosecutor had no prepared script. Roseman at least was able to confer with William Garth, his young associate, who suggested new lines of questioning to follow. O'Boy had to perform alone.

The prosecutor's first priority was to get Cole to retreat somewhat from his generous assessment of Altschule. The defense witness had a "first-class reputation as an internist," Cole explained, but "I think he was not given the facilities to do as careful and thorough a job as he would have liked in this case." Did he mean the CAT-scan, Dwyer asked. "Yes," said Cole. "If I were to have done the evaluation, I would have liked a much more extensive and organically focused battery of psychological tests, more extensive EEG, CAT-scan . . . I would have liked to consult with a neurologist before." He dismissed his colleague's procedure as "a very new and not clinically applied method." Altschule's interpretation was but "a speculative hypothesis supported by a little evidence."

Altschule was not surprised by Cole's hostility toward his thesis. "He'd never heard of it before. Jonathan Cole is a professor, and you cannot tell a professor anything he never heard of before, it's the nature of the animal." Roseman tried to make this point as he cross-examined the prosecutor's witness a second time. Could Cole conclude "beyond a reasonable doubt" that Charles was not substantially incapacitated at the time of the crime? O'Boy objected, and Dwyer upheld him. Expert witnesses need not be convinced beyond reasonable doubt, and, the judge added, that was "an unfair burden to place on any scientist." Roseman changed his question and got his answer anyway: The psychiatrist had no doubt that Charles's behavior was due to ordinary inebriation.

Having set Cole up, Roseman moved in to knock him down. "Is there anything in this statement that you can find," demanded the lawyer, "in which Miss Sussman said Mr. Decker was inebriated?"

"I guess one gets back to the definition of inebriation."

"I asked you a simple question," Roseman shot back. He repeated the question.

"Yes," replied Cole, "his violent behavior."

"You mean one cannot engage in violent behavior unless one is inebriated?"

"No, but when drinking beer, smoking marijuana, and engaging in violent behavior, it is a fair inference the alcohol contributed to the violent behavior." They had come a long way from scientific certitude.

Roseman returned the prosecutor's battered witness to him for yet another round of direct examination. O'Boy knew his expert's credibility had been impaired, but he still believed the facts were on his side. The very testimony Roseman had cited, he reminded Cole, indicated that the defendant had consumed eight or nine cans of beer, plus part of another quart. How would that affect his opinion? "I think it increases my comfort with my prior judgment," replied the grateful psychiatrist.

Roseman took one last crack. He had done as much as he could to discredit Cole's opinions, he thought, so he used the opportunity to reinforce the credibility of his own expert and his expert's scientific procedures. Was Cole familiar with the depressant effect of alcohol on the secretion of insulin? "In all fairness I was not aware of the specific effects," replied the psychiatrist, "but I'll be happy to take Dr. Altschule's word for it." What about Altschule's tests? Could Cole dispute them? "I assume that he is biochemically careful and that these are reliable and reasonable tests. I would like to have known more about the degrees of variability among a large range of subjects," Cole replied. Was Altschule, by reputation, a reliable investigator? "Yes."

The prosecution's expert witness was dismissed, and hurried home to Brookline.

*

Mark Altschule had remained in the courtroom to hear all of Jonathan Cole's testimony. Now called back to the stand for cross-examination, Altschule had his chance to defend himself.

O'Boy began his questioning by pursuing the connections between the defendant's apparent disease and his admitted history of drinking. Altschule was careful to answer each question as narrowly as possible, but the prosecution kept after the witness and finally got him to concede that Charles would not have suffered from Korsakoff's syndrome if he had not drunk alcohol. O'Boy then sparred with Altschule over how much beer the defendant had drunk on the particular night of the attack. "Three cans," the witness suggested. The prosecutor raised the number to eight. Concluding this line of questioning, O'Boy had Altschule admit that Charles had been drinking of his "own free will."

Having thus attacked the legal relevance of the physician's testimony, O'Boy proceeded to suggest that it was scientifically inconclusive as well. He did so by attempting to undermine each of the three legs upon which Altschule's theory of the case was based: the diagnosis of limbic damage (Korsakoff's syndrome), the presence of the unknown substance, and the nature of the assault.

He first tried to discredit Altschule's finding of Korsakoff's syndrome by bringing out the fact that Charles's psychiatric evaluation at Bridgewater had not detected the condition, but Altschule reminded him — and the court — that a state medical team had made the initial diagnosis, and that the defense witness had merely confirmed it. O'Boy then took another tack, building on Cole's criticism of the lack of physical evidence, such as EEGs and CAT-scans, to support Altschule's interpretation of the retained-information test.

"Would you agree with me that they would have been useful diagnostic tools to determine whether it was still there?" he asked.

"Absolutely," said Altschule.

"But you didn't order those tests, Doctor?"

"I would like you to ask me why," he told O'Boy irritably.

The prosecutor was inexorable: "Yes or no."

"No, I didn't."

The judge stepped in to calm the witness. "The other lawyer's going to ask you that," he told Altschule.

"Absolutely," agreed Roseman.

With that, the prosecutor turned to the second leg of Altschule's testimony, the presence of the unknown substance in Charles's blood and its relationship to drinking and violence. "If his wife were to testify that she had been with him a period of several years," he said, "and that he was never violent during that period and always very quiet, would that square with your diagnosis in this case?" (In fact, O'Boy did intend to call Pamela Decker to the stand.) Altschule explained that while he would have expected some sort of aberrant behavior before the assault, that could include any socially inappropriate actions, and these need not have taken violent form.

Rather than attempting to use this rather dubious answer to cast doubt on the existence of a chronic disorder, O'Boy suddenly reversed his field. Referring to Altschule's examination of Charles's insulin dysfunction seven years before, a condition associated with his drinking, the prosecutor asked, "If there were other instances in his past where it caused aberrant or violent behavior after drinking alcohol, would that have been a signal to him, Doctor, that the alcohol triggered this response?" Altschule made a qualified affirmative reply.

O'Boy then jumped quickly from the abstract to the specific: "Did you receive a history of other violent attacks by this individual, or violent behavior?"

"No violent attacks," returned Altschule, patently evading the other half of the question.

Mindful of the trial lawyers' precept that goes "Never ask a question unless you know the answer," O'Boy chose not to grill Altschule over whether he knew of any other violent behavior on Charles's part. In a sense, the prosecutor had no need to nail the point down, for he had structured his argument so that he would be a winner either way. If Charles had no apparent history of aberrant behavior, the diagnosis of brain lesions was brought into doubt. But if he had, then he should have been aware that alcohol was a trigger, and thus should assume the risk of losing self-control.

O'Boy closed his examination of Altschule's experimental findings with a question about their therapeutic relevance. "Is it your opinion, Doctor, that if he refrains from drinking alcohol then he will have no further problems with Korsakoff's syndrome or limbic-lobe damage and violent reactions that derive therefrom?"

"I certainly can't promise that," replied Altschule. "No."

Judge Dwyer, understandably concerned about the prognosis for the defendant, interjected, "Did I misunderstand your earlier testimony that without drinking you would not expect that this disease would revive itself so as to be calculated to cause aberrant behavior?"

"Without drinking, Korsakoff's should go away," Altschule answered, "but with respect to actual attacks, the trigger could be anything."

"Nonalcohol?"

"Yes."

"Like what?" persisted the judge.

"Like something internal," explained the witness. "If I may point to this"—he gestured toward a graph showing that the "unknown substance" in Charles's blood occurred even when he did not drink—"this is going up and down independently of anything, and I visualize that could do it."

O'Boy knew he had scored an important point in getting Altschule to hedge about the likelihood of Charles being dangerous in the future. He consolidated it with his main argument by having Altschule testify that four percent of the general population showed the same discrepant blood-alcohol readings. O'Boy hastened to put this abstract figure in concrete terms: "And out of, say, a city of a hundred thousand like New Bedford, you'd expect four thousand people to have this unknown substance?" Altschule conceded the number. Should all these people—and, presumably, over 200,000 more in Massachusetts, and 9,000,000 nationally—be excused for their crimes of violence because, like Charles Decker, they had an unknown substance in their blood? The prosecutor did not have to ask this question. No judge concerned about the broader impact of his decision would miss it.

Finally, O'Boy turned his attention to the third element in Altschule's diagnosis: the nature of the assault itself, as reported in the victim's testimony. Was it not true, he asked, that the attack had had two distinct phases, and lasted perhaps half an hour? The physician assented.

"So it wasn't a sudden flare-up, Doctor, that just as suddenly burned down; was it?" he demanded.

"If it was a sudden flare-up it didn't burn down instantaneously, no," Altschule agreed.

"It was a period of about half an hour, Doctor?" O'Boy repeated.

"Anyway, yes."

"And then afterwards, after the effects wore off or he sobered, so to speak"—O'Boy was still suggesting Charles had been drunk—"he took them—devised a rational plan to take these girls to where they'd be found. Is that correct?"

"Yes."

O'Boy had subtly shifted the questioning from medicine, Altschule's specialty, to crime, his own. He wound up his cross-examination with a series of hammer-blow attacks on the credibility of Altschule's interpretation of the assault. "Did you hear the testimony that this was a rural area where he attacked them?" he asked.

"Yes, sir."

"There was no one around?"

"Correct."

"Do you feel it significant, Doctor, that during this attack he took them to some place that was away from the road and away from people to commit the second attack with a rock on the girls?"

"I don't consider that significant, no sir."

"Do you consider that he was able to plan during the attack what would be a good place to continue his assault?"

"Well," replied Altschule, "I must explain about the nature of these attacks. They are formed and sequential, and some of them have the appearance of some organization."

"So there was some input from the cortex during that attack, wasn't there?" demanded the prosecutor.

"I wouldn't say that, no." The physician was slightly flustered.

O'Boy was pleased. He had scored a point on Altschule's turf. "That is all I have of this witness," he said.

*

"I will have to ask you the sixty-four-dollar question," Roseman told Altschule as he began his surrebuttal. "Why didn't you use that CAT-scan?"

"This whole procedure that I'm engaged in is not yet finished," replied the physician. "And I am still investigating something that has never been studied or described before. I don't know which way I'm going, trying this, trying that, and somewhere along the line I hope [to do] the CAT-scan and the EEG, but I'm doing so many other things on the subject I haven't been able to get to them." Moreover, Altschule continued, he did not think the CAT-scan would show anything, because the scattered areas of partially healed limbic lesion were too small to show up.

Roseman methodically used his redirect to shore up weaknesses that O'Boy's cross-examination had exposed. Yes, Altschule admitted, his research protocol was novel, but the enzyme and chromatograph tests were routine; other researchers had found discrepant readings in about four percent of their cases. The defense lawyer had his witness distinguish pathological intoxication, a term raised by the prosecution, from limbic attacks. The latter, Altschule explained, tend to be less organized, less directed, and longer lasting. Roseman covered several other technical points, chief among them the independent diagnosis of the defendant's Korsakoff's syndrome, and then sat down.

It was four in the afternoon, and Dwyer was ready to adjourn, but O'Boy had a few more questions. "I think you are on the fourth or fifth recross," the judge remarked wearily. The prosecutor would have done well to take the hint. He wanted to close strongly, but he miscalculated.

"Doctor," he began, "you said that the tests you took were the first tests of that kind that were ever performed. Is that correct?"

"I said the application of these methods of measurement to an alcohol-tolerance test were the first in the world as far as I knew," Altschule agreed.

"So Charles was an experiment?" (He could hardly have asked a more provoking question of this particular witness.)

"No, sir, he was my patient."

"A guinea pig?"

"Absolutely not, and I resent that."

The judge stepped in to soothe the furious physician: "I don't think he means it that way ... It was an unfortunate choice of words."

"I apologize," offered O'Boy. He was genuinely sorry, both personally ("I think I wounded the guy unnecessarily," he admits, though Altschule insists he was unscathed) and professionally (because the incident detracted from the impact he had made in his cross-examination).

"Very unfortunate," muttered Altschule, still ruffled.

"That concludes your testimony," Dwyer told him.

The prosecutor then told the court that one of his witnesses was no longer available, and asked for a stipulation—an agreement to accept evidence without proof (in this case, examination of the witness)—of the testimony he would have given. The statement of Charles Decker's employer indicated that Charles had worked at his nursery for six years. During that time he had always been very quiet and had never flared up in anger or violence even under provocation. Since turning eighteen the young man had generally drunk a couple of bottles of beer with his coworkers at the end of the day. He had done so on July 17, 1974, but had appeared sober when he left the nursery. Roseman checked the facts with his client, and agreed to the stipulation. There was one more witness to be called in the prosecution's rebuttal, but that would wait until the next day. The court recessed at 4:05.

At noon Wednesday, Pamela Decker took the stand where Gail Sussman had sat forty-eight hours earlier. The first witness had been frail and anxious, her hair still cropped in the aftermath of brain surgery. The last was voluptuous and confident. In Frank O'Boy's words, she looked like "something out of Mickey Spillane." This was Charles Decker's estranged wife, the mother of his child, the woman he had left at home to go riding with two schoolgirls—and the woman who had apparently been prepared to consign him to prison in order to get a divorce and custody of their daughter. What emotions lay behind her appearance to testify against him? And what evidence would she offer? O'Boy had met with her before the trial and was prepared to ask her about Charles's past behavior. She took the stand, was sworn in, and stared directly at her husband in the prisoner's dock. O'Boy had her give her name, and asked if she was the defendant's wife.

"Yes, I am," she replied. In view of that, Judge Dwyer told her, she could not be compelled to testify against him. Had that been explained to her? "Yes." Did she understand the law? "Yes."

"Notwithstanding that right you are desirous of testifying?" he went on.

She hesitated. "Yes."

"Is your answer yes?" asked the judge again.

"No," she replied at last. "No, I do not want to testify." O'Boy was startled by her last-minute decision. Pamela Decker was excused and quickly left the courtroom, her feelings and her knowledge about the defendant still concealed. To this day, O'Boy does not understand her sudden change of heart. He is thankful, however, that her appearance was not essential to proving his case.

*

There was one more person whose testimony had not been heard, though it could sway the outcome of the trial. David Roseman had no intention of calling his client to testify, but now his adversary approached the bench and offered as evidence Charles Decker's hospital records, including psychiatric interviews, from Bridgewater and Shattuck. Another round remained to be fought.

Roseman had seen the records, and knew he had to keep them from being introduced. They contained material that was potentially fatal to two key elements of the elaborately constructed defense case. First, Charles's own account of the events preceding the assault referred to provocation by the girls, information that compromised Altschule's diagnosis of an irrational, unprovoked limbic attack. Second, his client's psychiatric history made mention of earlier alcohol-related aggressive incidents, upsetting his argument on the volition issue. Other information on Charles's drinking, while not directly damaging to the defense case, certainly tended to support the prosecution.

No one could tell the score the judge was keeping in his mind. O'Boy felt that Jonathan Cole's testimony had been strong, but Roseman sensed that the defense had won the battle of experts, and that he was ahead on points. Now, at the end of the bout, O'Boy was winding up for a knockout blow.

The defense attorney could hardly claim that the hospital records were immaterial to the prosecution case. He could, however, argue that they were too relevant. They included, in several places, statements by the defendant that amounted to confessions of guilt.

No witness took the stand. No stonemason's hammers or chemistry charts were on display. It was a pure debate between Roseman and O'Boy, with Dwyer as the arbiter, over whether the law allowed admission of the hospital records. Armed with legal memoranda, the lawyers were ready to argue either nuances in the legislation or broad matters of public policy. The ultimate question was whether the judge, who soon would have to decide Charles Decker's guilt or innocence, would come to know as much about the case as the two lawyers who were presenting it.

Roseman invoked the Massachusetts statute barring admission of statements made by a defendant while under mandatory observation. O'Boy countered with a statutory exception for statements relating to a patient's mental and emotional condition. Roseman replied that the section was nullified by a separate provision barring admission of confessions. O'Boy responded that by claiming the assault itself was symptomatic of limbic dysfunction, the defense had implicitly conceded that Charles Decker had committed the crime.

Judge Dwyer finally realized that unless he knew what was in the records, he could not determine whether or not they were covered by the statutory exception dealing with mental condition. The judge asked O'Boy for an offer of proof.

An offer of proof is a procedure in which a judge hears proposed testimony off the record before ruling on its admissibility. In an ordinary jury trial, the panel is excused from the courtroom while the testimony is presented; if it is excluded, they never hear it. But in this case, Dwyer was acting as both judge and jury. He had to hear the evidence with one ear, while remaining deaf in the other. Frank O'Boy began to read.

"Do you want him to read this?" asked David Roseman, appalled.

"How else am I going to make the rulings?" demanded Dwyer. "Those are the fallacies of jury-waived cases sometimes, but I have to hear what the offer is so I can make the ruling." He was reminding the defense lawyer that the decision to waive a jury trial had been his own. "That's why I emphasized to you it is simply an offer and not being admitted before the court," the judge pointed out.

Finally, Charles Decker's own story was coming out. O'Boy read the first report of the Bridgewater psychiatrist: "This young man is alleged to have severely beaten two young girls. He admitted to me that he had done such. When asked why, he said that he did not know, only that after having drunk quite a bit, he stated several six-packs of beer, he went berserk. He further stated that he had done this before, beating up a young boy after having—"

"I would object!" Roseman interrupted. He had particularly feared two things in the hospital records, and this—his client's history of alcohol-linked outbursts—was perhaps the more damaging of them. Under the law on voluntary use of alcohol, by itself it could render the rest of his case irrelevant. He had to keep the judge from hearing this.

Dwyer turned on him angrily. "How am I going—"

"I withdraw that," said Roseman hastily. This was merely an offer of proof, not evidence. He could not object.

"I know these are troublesome things," Dwyer consoled him, "but you rely on a jury-waived judge, a trained lawyer, to exclude from his mind those things that are not going to be admitted in evidence."

"I apologize," said Roseman.

The judge was apologetic for his own anger. "I understand. It is commendable."

O'Boy read on, skimming the reports for statements that might constitute admissions of guilt. Two days after the crime, a psychotherapist had reported, "The patient admits he hit the two girls with a hammer on the head . . . He claims to have many problems but especially family, financial and work problems. He, however, denies any suicidal or homicidal thoughts. He denies any visual or auditory hallucinations." (These symptoms are characteristic of temporal-lobe epilepsy, which Mark and Ervin relate to limbic attack.)

O'Boy then read from a social worker's notes, written the same day: "Patient admits drinking large quantity of beer, smoking marijuana prior to this incident . . . The patient could give no reason for the assault . . . Patient claims he has excellent relationship with his entire family." (One facet of the "dyscontrol syndrome" is wife- and child-beating. This admission impaired any psychogenic-insanity argument as well.)

It was reported that at a diagnostic staff meeting two weeks later, Charles had "admitted he was intoxicated at the time of the alleged offense." Two days before that, he had again denied "auditory or visual hallucinations." A month after the crime, his examiners wrote: "He has been drinking since an early age, at least fourteen, and he has been a problem at home because of drinking excessively, creating difficulties, being violent at times to other children while intoxicated, and on at least one occasion neighbors had to restrain him by tying him until he quieted down during one of these alcoholic, violent outbursts of his. He admits to the above facts. He admits to normal sexual relations with his wife." (Abnormal sexual behavior characterizes the "dyscontrol syndrome.") Once again, the alcohol-violence link was established.

O'Boy came to the defendant's most complete account and started reading almost tonelessly. "He (being the defendant) claims he had drunk a considerable amount of alcohol the night of the alleged offense. Being already drunk, he was returning from Seekonk to Rehoboth from work when those two girls which he placed in mid-teens [who] were his neighbors, although they did not know him, asked him for a ride back home. Evidently before they reached home he claims they asked him to go and drink with him and maybe use drugs. He claims he dropped them off some place, went home to get marijuana and more liquor and bought more in the process.

"Then about one or two hours of drinking in his car in a deserted area, he claims to not have a clear recollection of the sequence of events which occurred, although he claims being directly under the influence of alcohol and drugs, him being completely under the influence of alcohol and drugs and the girls being almost in the same condition, although not as bad as him. They had arguments and fights. He claims the arguments ensued when they started to become annoysome, teasing him, daring him to come drink again with them the next day, teasing him and possibly threatening him that they might tell to his wife what they had been doing." (The prosecutor paused.)

"He claims in general he was very annoyed and upset, and that there was a scuffle. He attempted to dissuade them. They hit him first with the hammer which he had for professional landscape reasons in the back of his car. Evidently during the scuffle he disarmed them and started hitting them too." (This was provocation.)

"He failed to tell us how he has done many things which he claims he does not clearly remember without any specifications, being under the influence of drugs and alcohol; then automatically acted as a rather rational person by dropping the girls properly in front of this home, making sure the lights were on and that they would receive help and him taking off as he says in order to avoid further trouble; and how he went immediately home and told that to his wife, and how later on the same night following the suggestions of his parents he gave himself up to the police."

O'Boy turned a page and glanced at another report. "The next matter," he began, "is —"

Dwyer stopped him. "They are all of the same general nature?" he asked. Yes, responded the prosecutor, they were the same. He started to restate his view of their admissibility, but the judge cut him off again. He had heard enough.

"I am not inclined to give a hypertechnical interpretation of this statute, which is far from satisfactory from lawyers' points of view because of the apparent inconsistencies," Dwyer explained. "I think in the spirit of the legislation I am obliged to recognize that a patient committed to a mental hospital by a court is clothed with a certain amount of protection..." He had accepted the defense argument. "So in view of that," he concluded, "I am going to exclude all of it."

David Roseman hoped the judge's mind was as clear as the record.

*

With no jury in the box and a strong judge on the bench, lawyers' closings lose much of their importance. They are no longer the occasion for those forensic fireworks that turn defeat into victory in so many pulp novels and television programs. Instead, the closing provides an opportunity for each side to present its theory of the case, to hone the arguments forged in hours of questions and answers. Counsel may hammer home a few points, and deflect a few more, but the facts are already on the table.

In its presentation of the case, the defense follows and responds to the charges of the prosecution. For closing arguments, the order is reversed. David Roseman began by saying, "I think it's fair to say the issue in this lawsuit is the issue of responsibility, criminal responsibility of the defendant Charles Decker at the time of the alleged act." His goal, therefore, would be to show "that there was a reasonable doubt as to his responsibility."

To outline his argument, he ran through the witnesses one by one, in the order of their appearance. Gail Sussman, he stated, had described "three young people" simply "engaging in some social conversation, some social drinking...riding somewhat aimlessly on a summer evening." Then this commonplace scene was shattered by "an unprovoked, unpremeditated attack which seemed to have come out of the sky." He pointed out that the victim's testimony had described his client as entirely sober, then suddenly "scary," and finally, just as suddenly, childlike and remorseful. The courts, he added, recognized that in some cases a crime itself could be diagnostic of an illness (though he agreed with the judge that this was pushing the argument further).

Then he proceeded to Mark Altschule, the "treating physician" who had taken charge of Charles's care. (There was an overt comparison with Cole here, and a subliminal argument for acquittal.) It was Altschule who had understood the bizarre assault as a limbic attack. He had also confirmed the limbic lesion, Korsakoff's syndrome, in Charles Decker's brain. Roseman briefly defended the medical reasoning here, but above all he told the judge, "I ask you to accept the diagnosis on the basis of the man, his experience, his training, and his general knowledge in this area."

Finally (the third leg of Altschule's argument) there were the blood tests, revealing that Charles Decker suffered from an alcohol-metabolism abnormality that for years had pumped an unknown, but probably toxic, substance into his system. At this point, Dwyer raised a question. Why, he asked, did the defense lawyer insist on having it both ways? Why did he contend both that his client had been sober and that alcohol had triggered his client's condition? Roseman tried to pass off the discrepancy, but the judge would have none of it. Could it be, he suggested, that Roseman wanted "the alcoholic trigger for the Korsakoff's syndrome" but feared "our traditional law in this Commonwealth that the voluntary use of intoxicating liquor is not a defense"?

"Not at all," answered the lawyer. He had no such fear, for his client had not been drunk, he explained. But Dwyer pressed, and Roseman launched into the argument he had prepared. In the case of an unexpected, indeed unknown condition, caused by a long-term metabolic abnormality—even one involving alcohol—then "the traditional rule of voluntary ingestion really makes no play."

"That is a hard argument that you advance," the judge commented. How, he wanted to know, could drinking be involuntary? Roseman explained his theory: The drinking per se was voluntary, of course, but his client had not been in voluntary control of its unexpected consequences. Moreover, he added, the evidence indicated that the immediate trigger of any given attack might not be alcohol.

It was, he admitted, "a unique set of facts and a unique diagnosis. But I argue to you it is a well-founded medical opinion." The judge, he noted, had understood that Altschule worked deductively. "And," he went on, "I suppose at any stage one cannot say you arrive at the absolute science of the truth; that is for philosophers. But he did offer to you the product of what he had done."

Mark Altschule, Roseman continued, "has attempted to establish medical as opposed to psychiatric reasons to explain the behavior." Roseman suggested that that alone explained Cole's rejection of Altschule's theory. "Dr. Cole," he stressed, "is a psychiatrist. This kind of analysis, I argue to you, is absolutely foreign to a person like Dr. Cole." Altschule's work was not an "illusory" science like psychiatry: His approach was "diametrically opposite, deductive to be sure, but it has been on the basis of medical deductions, the basis of medical tests administered by a man, I think, of unquestioned credentials."

The defense, David Roseman concluded, was not seeking an easy solution. Charles Decker should not simply be released. He should remain under the court's jurisdiction, and undergo further tests to define his problem. But the defense had shown that there was reasonable doubt as to his responsibility. He should be found innocent.

The case Frank O'Boy surveyed looked very different. It was focused on a single issue: "Did alcohol trigger a reaction that caused the act that happened in that car on Brook Street in Rehoboth and in that field that evening?" If it did, then Charles Decker was responsible under the law. O'Boy saw the weak links in Roseman's chain of reasoning, and he hammered at them.

Whatever interpretations were imposed on the defendant's actions on the night of July 17, 1974, whatever explanations were advanced for his sudden assault, he reminded the judge, there was one fact on which all agreed. "He did drink quite a bit of alcohol that night, and it was a voluntary act." It was, moreover (here he relied on a scrap of information salvaged from the excluded hospital records), the act of a man diagnosed as sane—but afflicted with a problem of alcohol and drug abuse.

As for Altschule's unknown substance—O'Boy called it Brand X—should the court accept a novel defense, one that would be available to four percent of the population, on the basis of a one-shot experiment? Or should it stand with Dr. Cole and "mainstream psychiatric opinion," and reject this speculative theory? He cited legal precedents holding that "the judicial acceptance of a scientific theory can occur only when it follows a general acceptance by the community of scientists involved." The physician's behavioral diagnoses, too, were unconvincing and contradicted by other authorities, O'Boy maintained. There was no reason here to overturn a hundred years of Massachusetts law.

The defense's medical case, O'Boy urged, failed to meet the irresponsibility standard set forth in *McHoul*. The necessary link between the act and the alleged reason for the act had not been demonstrated. And because voluntarily consumed alcohol was involved, neither had the connection between the reason and the claim of criminal irresponsibility. The prosecution had presented its own psychiatric testimony that showed that the defendant was responsible. Under the circumstances, O'Boy concluded, "the finding of this case by the court should be guilty on all of the charges."

Judge Thomas E. Dwyer had a few questions for the prosecutor, and a few procedural details to settle. He glanced down at the briefs the lawyers had filed. Then he looked up. "I want to compliment counsel, and I rarely do this, for an extremely well-prepared case on both sides, including the assistant counsel for the defense," he said, acknowledging William Garth's contribution. "I think you have been extremely helpful to the court, and your patience of course has been tested. This is a very short case, now in its third day, but I want to compliment you on the record."

Both lawyers thanked him. It was Dwyer's case now.

# 6. Judgment

JUDGE DWYER ASKED everyone to come forward to the bench, not just the lawyers—Frank O'Boy, David Roseman, and Roseman's associate—but the defendant Charles Decker, his father Nicholas, and his physician, Mark Altschule.

"It is an extremely difficult case," the judge told them. "It is one that has caused me more concern than probably any case I can remember since I have been a judge. The issue is very simple: whether I should follow the recommendation of the D.A. and send this man away to jail for a long while, or whether, on the other hand, we think he is rehabilitatable. And whether or not he constitutes no further risk to the community."

The judge had already announced one decision: He had found Charles Decker guilty of two counts (one for each victim) of attempted murder and two counts of assault and battery with a dangerous weapon. He had "negatived the claim of criminal irresponsibility," but he added that "at the same time I am not oblivious to the fact that there is a serious problem lurking here, even though it may not have amounted to the dignity of a legal defense."

Though not enough to save Charles from conviction, the medical evidence Roseman and Altschule had presented still might have a bearing on the judge's sentence. Dwyer had broad discretion. He could completely suspend whatever sentence he imposed, or he could commit Charles to Walpole, the state's maximum-security prison, where he would not even be eligible for parole for at least six years.

It was one week after Mark Altschule had stepped down from the witness stand in the same New Bedford courtroom. Judge Dwyer had taken the case under advisement so that he could review the evidence and the lawyers' requests for legal rulings before rendering his decision. Now the clerk had read the judgment, and Dwyer had called for the Commonwealth's recommendation on sentencing.

"Your Honor please," said O'Boy, "the assault which the defendant committed on the two victims in this case — a hair-breadth from causing a double homicide — I don't think, short of murder, a case could have been more serious. However, Your Honor, looking at the defendant's background, the nature of the crime, the Commonwealth feels that in this case that justice should be tempered with mercy in the form of a sentence that would allow rehabilitation of the defendant after a period of incarceration, yet hold a club so to speak over the defendant."

O'Boy recommended a sentence of eighteen years and a day at the Concord Reformatory, a medium-security prison. Charles would be eligible for parole after two years, and he would be credited with the time he had already served at Bridgewater and Shattuck. O'Boy also asked that the court recommend to the parole board that if Charles was released, he be placed on strict probation to keep him off alcohol.

Roseman was relieved, but he still fought to keep his client out of jail. Responding to the prosecution's suggestion, he told Judge Dwyer, "Your Honor, I have heard the recommendation of Mr. O'Boy, and I understand the spirit in which it was given. I, however, still strongly urge that what you have here, especially for the purposes of disposition, is a medical problem." The lawyer reminded the court that Charles had already served almost a full year in prison — Dwyer interrupted to ask for the specific dates — and that Nicholas Decker had not pledged the family home as bail until the medical studies had indicated that Charles "would no longer be a menace" to himself or anyone else.

"It is anticipated," Roseman stated, "that within the next several weeks, and I would say two to three weeks, I can't guarantee it, when a bed is available, Mr. Decker will be admitted to the metabolic ward, Beth Israel Hospital, to be subjected to further and other tests administered by Dr. Altschule." The purpose of this testing would be to identify the unknown substance and to see if it could be eliminated or controlled. Left unsaid but nonetheless very clear was the fact that the tests would be performed only if the judge agreed to suspend Charles's sentence. "I do not think," Roseman concluded, "it is in the interest of justice, or in the interest of society, or even in the interest of those poor girls, to subject him to further confinement, given the nature of his medical problem."

It was after Roseman had finished his appeal that Judge Dwyer asked everyone to come forward. Charles Decker, his father, Dr. Altschule, and the lawyers clustered near the witness stand. "I have called you up here," Dwyer said, "because I want to say to you the deep concern I have in this case. This morning I disposed of another case where having read the probation report, I indicated that it was the most unpromising report I've read in my career as a judge. I have read this probation report—probably the most promising report I've ever read as a judge."

Dwyer noted the favorable circumstances, among them a talented and supportive family and a wide range of medical services available to treat Charles. He mentioned that he had conferred independently with a psychiatrist—not, he added, about the finding of guilt, but about possible treatment beyond what Altschule and Nicholas Decker had in mind. He would refer the defendant to the Human Resources Institute for a psychological work-up. "It probably will be expensive, although it has been indicated, and I don't vouch for this, that insurance may cover it. All the resources of the Commonwealth of which I can command will be used to assist in that regard." Dwyer also mentioned a physician at McLean who specialized in temporal-lobe epilepsy. "Now, I like the approach suggested, Beth Israel Hospital, namely, further pursuance of the identification of a nonidentified factor in the blood. Anything you people want to may be done. I don't mean to get in the way of that at all. I'm not following that course. I have problems of conscience in disposing of this matter in justice to both sides."

Dwyer, who moments earlier had seemed ready to impose a jail term, now seemed inclined not to do so. Perhaps he had been swayed by Roseman's plea; he certainly had been impressed by the medical program the lawyer had outlined. But the degree to which he had taken the initiative, the details he had already worked out, suggest that his earlier attitude may simply have been intended to impress upon the defense the seriousness of the situation. Moreover, while Dwyer wished to see the tests done, he still was not ready to make a final decision on jailing Charles. Specifically, he wanted the Human Resources Institute to report whether "this patient [a choice of words that suggested things were now going Roseman's way] can with therapy competently handle himself in the community." He added, "That's the kind of language I understand vis-à-vis a criminal charge."

The judge also said that he wanted to see a more thorough investigation of Charles's family situation. He was particularly concerned with the defendant's long history of drinking. Roseman assured the judge that as far as he knew, Charles had had no drugs or alcohol since his release from Bridgewater, other than what Altschule had administered in the tests. Charles's father, Nicholas, volunteered that he was positive his son had done no drinking. "The simple measure—the simple measure that has been held over my son since Dr. Altschule and his colleagues informed me that they could no longer discern the lesion—was the recognition of the fact that he would go back to Bridgewater instantly, because I would go over and revoke his bail," Nicholas Decker said.

"The best therapy in the world," agreed the judge.

"He knows it would be applied," continued Decker, "and that every member of the family stood behind me in this respect."

"If there is the slightest deviation from it, you should inform the court, because we are all trying to help," said Dwyer. "No one is trying to hurt."

Roseman, seeing that the judge was impressed with the father's attitude, let Decker carry the ball. "May I add further, the burden on me, the reason I took that stand, was from my knowledge of the problem," the scientist continued. "These two girls were unfortunate. It could have been his wife, could have been his mother. It could have been anyone. And as a consequence, you don't play with that situation. That was our position."

Dwyer announced that he would continue the case thirty days to allow for the investigation he had outlined, before making a decision on sentencing. If the psychological and family studies could not be done, he noted, "then we better readjust our sights." Charles had won a stay of execution, but the judge made it clear that he was not ruling out jail sentence, perhaps even a longer one than O'Boy had proposed. He did not want to scare anybody, he said, but "everyone knows, of course, that the judge is not bound by the recommendation. Everyone knows what the maximum penalty is involved in these offenses."

The case was called again in early June, this time in the Taunton court where the probable-cause hearing had been held almost two years earlier. In April the weather had been cold and raw, but now the trees were lush and the air warm. David Roseman was optimistic. Although Altschule had not been able to conduct the promised series of blood tests at Beth Israel, virtually everything else Judge Dwyer had asked for had been done. A psychiatrist at the Human Resources Institute had seen Charles and written a helpful letter. The probation office had done an unusually thorough investigation and recommended favorably. Charles's old employer had asked him to come back to work full time. If Judge Dwyer leaned toward suspending sentence, the developments of the last month were justification enough.

The probation report filled in some aspects of Charles Decker's background that had not been within Dr. Altschule's domain. The report stated, "The home visit indicates that the parents are concerned and supportive of their son despite all of his past difficulties." The report added, however, "This concern appears to be exhibited in the form of financial support and living accommodations rather than through feelings and affections." Perhaps most revealing, it noted, "The father seems to see his son's present difficulties as the result of a medical problem and minimizes the possibility of family or individual difficulties. This does not appear to be a problem for Charles, since he seems to see himself in a clearer and more realistic fashion."

By commending Charles's self-awareness, the report implied that Nicholas Decker's single-mindedness not only might be excessive, but might create difficulty between father and son. Yet though the report noted the interpersonal dimensions of the situation, it certainly did not reject the medical implications the defense had raised. Indeed, when the probation official who wrote the report summarized his recommendations, he urged that the biochemical testing continue. "I think that is not only an absolute necessity for the defendant, but I think it would be very helpful for those of us who deal with drug abuse and alcohol abuse so that we will know a little better how that affects the mind," he wrote.

Judge Dwyer turned to the prosecutor for his comments. O'Boy did not quarrel with the probation report, but he noted that the question it addressed essentially was whether punishment would help the defendant. O'Boy reminded the court that there was another important consideration at stake: "the public's right to expect that perpetrators of serious crimes when found guilty must do some period of incarceration."

In another case, O'Boy might have sought imprisonment not just on grounds of retribution but also on the basis of the public's need to be protected. Charles had, after all, proved his capacity for violence. The prosecutor deliberately avoided this tack, however, aware that the record here was at best ambiguous. If Altschule was correct, his patient's problem was under control. Moreover, Dr. Levy, the psychiatrist with the Human Resources Institute, had written that he regarded Charles as a good prospect for rehabilitation. Levy had cautioned that "psychiatrists have a poor batting average" in predicting recurrence of criminal behavior, but had gone on to note that Charles did not come from a violent background, that he had coped well with confinement at Bridgewater, and that he now had strong support from his family and through his job. The prosecution had to rest its argument for a jail sentence on the gravity of the crime, a fact beyond dispute.

Roseman responded by emphasizing that since his release, Charles had been living in a stable environment with his parents and now had responsibility for his young daughter. The answer, he contended, was the strictest form of probation, whereas sending the defendant to prison would be "the wrong thing at the wrong time." Charles, he noted, had already been confined in Bridgewater State Hospital for almost a year.

"May I see the probation report on him?" Judge Dwyer asked. The clerk handed him the file. "I just want to refresh my recollection from the blue sheet." Roseman, O'Boy, Altschule, and the two Deckers watched as the judge studied the papers. He drew one page close to him, wrote on it, then handed it back to the clerk of courts without saying a word.

"Charles Decker," the clerk read, "on these various indictments, 48732, 48733, 48734, 48735, the court having found you guilty of these matters, it is the order of the court that you be punished by confinement in the Massachusetts Correctional Institution at Concord for a term of eighteen years and one day—execution of this sentence suspended and you are placed on probation for a term of six years."

Charles had been spared jail. There was a long list of probation conditions—abstinence from drugs and alcohol, continued counseling, full-time employment, random screening for drug and alcohol use—but Roseman, speaking for his client, had already accepted these measures. Nevertheless, Judge Dwyer himself read aloud each of the conditions, making sure that the defendant, his family, and the probation officer understood their rigor. He also took the unusual step of retaining jurisdiction over the case in the future, as he would necessarily be more familiar with the situation than would any other judge. In closing, Dwyer looked down at the defendant and asked him, "Is there any ambiguity, any misunderstanding you have, Mr. Decker?"

Charles Decker, whose violent and peculiar actions had been chronicled, whose brain had been scrutinized, whose future had been in the balance, but who had been mute throughout the trial, answered, "No, sir."

*

Judge Dwyer's decision settled the legal issue of criminal responsibility in the case of Charles Decker by ruling the young man guilty of assault and attempted murder. At the same time, however, the suspended sentence recognized that the scientific aspect of the case remained unresolved, and made provision for further research. The immediate goal of the studies ordered by the judge was the determination and treatment of the defendant's individual condition, rather than a general investigation of violence-inducing metabolic defects.

The specific tests upon which the judge insisted proved negative; neither a CAT-scan nor additional EEGs provided clear evidence of brain dysfunction in Charles Decker. Additional tolerance tests, with variations, refined the earlier findings without significantly changing the overall picture. Altschule was able to confirm his belief that his patient's eating habits as well as his drinking played a part in bringing on an abnormal reaction. During all the testing, however, the physician never actually induced an episode of violence like the one that had led to the trial. He believes that the change in Charles's lifestyle, brought about by incarceration and the conditions of the parole, may have diminished the condition generally, as it apparently did the Korsakoff's syndrome.

Because there is evidence of a genetic component in Korsakoff's syndrome and in many other physiological abnormalities, the physician conducted similar tests on Charles's brothers. None showed an untoward reaction to alcohol, even after fasting. Altschule plans to repeat the tests, this time administering insulin as well, but he acknowledges that hereditary factors are so complex that negative results are by no means conclusive.

One area in which progress has been made is the identification of the "unknown substance." The first ultrasensitive chromatographic analysis, arranged through Prof. Sanford Miller and his associates at the Massachusetts Institute of Technology, detected only 1,3-butanediol, the more common and benign isomer. Even more precise tests, however, vindicated Altschule's initial conjecture that 2,3-butanediol was present, although they also found at least four other unusual compounds.

These limited findings have strengthened Altschule's belief that he understands the general mechanism behind his patient's condition. When the young man suffers a hypoglycemic attack (which may be triggered by alcohol), his body deals with the blood-sugar deficit by drawing upon the fats stored in its tissues. The process by which the body metabolizes any particular substance involves a complex and specific series of enzymatic actions, each of which must occur in its proper order if the function is to proceed normally. In Charles Decker's body, Altschule argues, an abnormality in the metabolism of certain fat, not yet identified, allows butanediol to remain in his system without being broken down into less toxic products. According to the physician, Charles "certainly generates, by his own little self, a poison when he doesn't have his breakfast."

A well-known example of a simple metabolic disorder with serious consequences is phenylketonuria (PKU), a genetically transmitted condition leading to mental retardation. Children affected by PKU lack a liver enzyme that acts on phenylalanine. As a result, this ordinarily nutritious amino acid, found in eggs and milk, builds up in their bodies and poisons them. Newborn infants are now routinely tested for PKU. The parents need only soak a card in the child's urine, let it dry, and mail it to a laboratory. If the condition is detected—that is, if the enzyme is missing—its ill effects can be averted, principally by avoidance of foods containing phenylalanine.

In regard to treatment of his patient, Mark Altschule is sanguine in principle but less confident in practice. First of all, he will need to identify the particular fat whose metabolism produces the toxic substance. Altschule thinks that the culprit is probably an unsaturated vegetable fat, the kind found in margarine, for instance, but this is far from certain. Once the fat is identified, he is sure that a chemical therapy can be found that will inhibit its breakdown; but the side effects could be serious. As for encouraging the young man to eat regularly, fifty years of medical practice have taught him that such an approach is almost hopeless: "You can't make a fellow eat his breakfast if he doesn't feel like eating it."

Sanford Miller, now chief scientist at the Food and Drug Administration's Bureau of Foods, believes his colleagues' interpretation of the process may be oversimplified. "They had a very important observation by the tail," he avers, "but they were looking for a 'magic bullet.'" To Miller, it does not seem reasonable to conclude that the butanediol—even in toxic form—was the direct cause of the mental symptoms. Rather, he thinks the abnormal metabolite was "probably a reflection of a more complex metabolic problem." In that case, a full understanding of the condition, and development of a treatment, may be even farther away. For Charles Decker, in one respect any remedy may come too late. Altschule believes that "the presence of this substance in his blood over a period of time has caused his mental function to deteriorate. I think he's become simple."

After his conviction, Charles Decker continued to live with his parents in Rehoboth. Though the tests and other conditions imposed by his probation circumscribed his activities, he returned to full-time work at the nursery. Pamela Decker won an uncontested divorce, but dropped her petition for custody of their daughter, who thus remained with her father and grandparents. Charles found a girl friend. Gradually his supervision was relaxed, and he reestablished a more normal way of life.

In early 1979, more than two and a half years after his trial, police in Pawtucket, Rhode Island, responding to a report of a disturbance, arrested Charles Decker. It was initially suspected that he had been drinking (a violation of the terms of his suspended sentence), but Charles managed to persuade his probation officer that his slurred speech had been the product of his disease, not drunkenness. According to William Garth, the lawyer who represented him in this proceeding, "the presence of butanediol in the body can produce an odor of cheap sherry." The court did not revoke his probation but did reimpose the urine-monitoring program, which had been allowed to lapse. He was now working only occasionally. Two years later the young man, now nearing thirty, was arrested again, this time for an episode involving an alleged threat of violence against a friend. Once more, he was first thought to have been drinking. And once more, Charles managed to have his probation continue and to avoid jail. Nevertheless, these incidents suggest that today, no less than on July 17, 1974, Charles Decker's personal future remains shadowed by doubt.

Yet Mark Altschule argues that "given the patterns of what we know about medicine, namely its diversity, and the infinite complexity of its interrelations, what has grown out of this boy's experience may in time, in $x$ number of decades, have a very broad influence on medicine, and especially the medicine of behavior." Whether or not Charles Decker's case has broader importance will depend on the investigations it inspires into both the mechanism of the metabolic process and its implications in terms of societal violence.

Altschule has acted as a sort of clearing-house for clinical studies aimed at determining the prevalence and nature of the condition. "Since I know all about it, as much as is known," he explains, "people naturally come to me saying, 'What shall we do next?'" And he adds, "I would like to have a lot of people working on it, as that way I don't have to."

Among the projects in which the physician is interested or involved are studies of alcoholics conducted in Rhode Island and Pennsylvania. In one of these tests, two-thirds of the subjects turned out to have the still-mysterious residue in their blood-streams. In another, the incidence was lower, but it appeared to correlate with independent diagnoses of manic-depressive illness, which in turn has been vaguely linked to both abnormal butanediol and violent behavior. An especially interesting study is getting under way in Alaska. It was begun when a public defender there, struck by the apparent fact that Native Americans show an unusual propensity to become violent after drinking alcohol, suggested that research might reveal a physiological explanation.

As it stands today, general scientific knowledge of the condition parallels Judge Dwyer's conclusion from the evidence presented to him five years ago in the Decker case. There does seem to be some sort of physiological condition that poses a violent threat to society. Further research is clearly desirable. For the moment, however, there is no certainty as to the precise nature of the problem, and no cure.

Altschule believes that the abnormality is fairly common. When he lectures on the Decker case, as he occasionally does, members of the audience often approach him afterward to describe their own similar experiences. Altschule cautions against the very tendency to leap to conclusions that some attribute to him. "One of the things that any well-trained clinician would know—there is no one-to-one relationship between any physiological or chemical finding and any clinical condition. A physiological finding will have various clinical manifestations, and a single chemical condition will have various causes. So you cannot assume that every person who behaves peculiarly after missing breakfast is going to have this condition."

According to the physician, widespread failure to understand this basic fact (a failure actually institutionalized in the scientific community) is a major impediment to thorough investigation of the medical issues raised by this case. The studies in which he is involved are clinical studies, he explains. Though they use laboratory data, their objective is to develop a clinical concept. "Now that is unfashionable," Altschule says. "Today you have to have an explanation, otherwise your paper probably won't get published."

The peer review system, under which scientific grants are awarded and articles published according to the recommendations of other researchers in the same field, is at the root of the problem, according to Altschule. The most common complaint about the system, though one refuted by several studies, is that it favors well-known names over projects that have real merit.

Altschule's complaint goes deeper. He argues that peer review hinders scientific progress by discouraging research that does not fit in with current knowledge or dominant theories. "You know," he remarks, "Louis Pasteur would never get a grant."

Altschule himself, as a matter of fact, has never held a grant from a government agency. He has had government contracts, which are not subject to peer review. Nicholas Decker, who shares Altschule's opinions on this subject, also avoids peer review, by working directly for a federal research facility, which he claims affords him more freedom than an academic post would. Those who oppose the peer review system cannot simply be relegated to the lunatic fringe of science. Rosalyn Yalow, the medical physicist and Nobel Prize winner, agrees: "What happens is a group of peers look at the experiment you're planning and, if it's like the experiments they want to do, they understand it and frequently fund it." Altschule's formulation of the issue is somewhat different. "I have no peers," he says. "This doesn't necessarily mean I'm superior—but only that I'm different."

This question of the sociology of medical research was raised explicitly in the trial of Charles Decker. David Roseman, in his closing argument, asserted the validity of Altschule's empirical clinical studies, and suggested that the prosecution's expert, Jonathan Cole, could not appreciate their value because he was a prisoner of psychiatric orthodoxy. Frank O'Boy, rebutting him, stood firmly with Cole and scientific consensus. Yet the direct confrontation was between lawyers, not scientists; and the court's decision was a decision of law, not of science. In the end the law, imperious in its domain, took what it needed from each side.

To some extent it may be said that in arriving at this resolution, the law—in the person of Judge Dwyer—was reconciling what its own adversary process had torn apart. Despite the courtroom confrontation of the two expert witnesses, and despite their real differences of opinion, neither of them can be said absolutely to represent one side or the other in the debate over psychogenic versus physiological causes of mental illness. Altschule is a lifelong opponent of glib psychoanalytic categorization, but he hardly denies that some problems are psychic in origin. Cole rejected Altschule's theory out of hand, but his own career is devoted to elucidating physical approaches to mental conditions.

No one today questions the fact that some mental effects have underlying physical causes. Syphilis, once a leading cause of mental illness, is now known to be the result of infection by a spirochete. Pellagra, another once-widespread disease with mental manifestations, arises from a nutritional deficiency (as do Wernicke's disease and Korsakoff's syndrome). The proverbial madness of hatters, still a common simile in an era in which the occupation is virtually extinct, was an effect of the chemicals used in the trade. Similarly, the relationship between limbic disorders and uncontrollable violence is thoroughly accepted in medical and psychiatric circles — in principle at least, and sometimes in practice.

When a sudden personality change follows an identifiable brain injury or disease, even the most orthodox Freudian may offer a diagnosis of posttraumatic brain syndrome. In 1956, a twenty-year-old Connecticut man, driving around the countryside with his girl friend, inexplicably turned on her and killed her. This was the culmination of a series of violent outbursts that had begun when he was thirteen, after a bout of St. Vitus' dance (chorea), a disease that affects the limbic area of the brain. The jury, weighing complex medical testimony, found him innocent by reason of insanity, and remanded him to a state hospital.

The most important difference between this case and that of Charles Decker almost two decades later is that the defendant's criminal behavior could be linked to a disease he had contracted, rather than to an innate condition. There is great resistance in our society to the idea that there is such a thing as a born criminal. At the same time, some writers have won wide acclaim by arguing that the entire human race is innately violent. The Nobel Prize–winning ethologist Konrad Lorenz, as well as such best-selling popular anthropologists as Robert Ardrey, Lionel Tiger, and Robin Fox, portray man as a "naked ape," whose aggressive tendencies are legacies from more primitive evolutionary ancestors. With little scientific backing, Arthur Koestler suggests the reverse: that the unprecedented elaboration of the human brain renders the outer cortex incapable of controlling the inner limbic brain, thus allowing war, murder, and other violence. (Harvard sociobiologist Edward O. Wilson, however, believes that the hypothalamic-limbic complex is the seat of altruism, the biological basis of society, as well as of aggression.)

Researchers in a number of fields have made tentative connections between subtle physical abnormalities and the propensity for violence. In one study, for example, seventy-three percent of murderers who had acted with no apparent motive were found to have unusual EEG tracings. Scientists are intrigued by the apparent association, but have yet to fathom the underlying mechanism.

The best-known recent attempt to define a physiological basis for criminality began in 1965, when Scottish researchers reported that a disproportionate number of criminally insane prisoners had abnormal sex chromosomes. Instead of showing the XY pair of ordinary men, their karyotypes revealed extra chromosomes in XYY, or more rarely XXY or XXYY, configurations. These "supermales" supposedly shared various characteristics, including tallness, low intelligence, and extreme aggressiveness.

The idea that tens or hundreds of thousands of these vicious natural criminals were at large in society led scientists to set up long-term studies, and caused law-enforcement officials to call for genetic screening. A French murderer won a reduced sentence because he was an XYY. In Australia, another murderer won an insanity verdict using such a chromosomal abnormality as one element of his defense. The most widely publicized XYY claim in the United States came in the case of Richard Speck, who had strangled and stabbed eight nurses in their Chicago dormitory in 1966. This time, the defense never got off the ground. Speck was tall, stupid, and vicious, but his chromosomes were normal.

Shortly thereafter, the entire supermale theory began to collapse. New studies produced conflicting results: XYY chromosomes were indeed associated with criminality, but not necessarily with violent crime. Moreover, the prevalence of the condition among criminals appeared to be much lower than earlier reports had indicated. A recent federal survey concluded that "there is insufficient evidence to support any policy decision" based on the XYY syndrome.

Yet there remains strong evidence of the influence of genetic factors in criminal behavior. Identical twins are known to be much more likely to share criminal records than are nonidentical siblings. More striking are the findings of a Danish study of adoptees. Among adopted men whose biological and adoptive fathers were both noncriminals, only ten percent had criminal records. For those whose adoptive fathers had criminal records while their biological fathers did not—that is, who might be inclined toward crime by environment rather than by heredity—the rate was scarcely higher. By contrast, biological sons of criminals, adopted and raised by noncriminals, became criminals themselves twice as often as did members of the other two groups.

These are statistical results. They indicate that something is there to be found, but they offer no clues as to what it is, except that it is genetically transmitted. Certainly they offer no assistance to the physician treating a patient, or to the lawyer defending a client. Meanwhile, on the molecular rather than the sociological level, a new approach to the study of the relationship between brain dysfunction and violent behavior has opened up as a result of recent advances in neurochemical research. In the past decade—indeed, since Charles Decker's trial—our understanding of the human brain has been revolutionized by the discovery of the role played by protein messengers known as endorphins. One class of endorphins, the enkaphalins, has been found to act on the limbic-system receptors that govern both emotional reactions and pain transmission. More tentatively, they have also been implicated in degenerative brain disease. As yet, however, no connection has been established between these physiological findings and the statistics suggesting inherited criminal tendencies, or between general scientific hypothesis and individual cases of violent behavior.

The difficulties inherent in bringing scientific generality to bear on particular medical or legal instances are exacerbated by the priorities that guide research. Mark Altschule admires the laboratory studies of alcohol metabolism being done by Richard Veech and his colleagues at the National Institute for Alcohol Abuse and Addiction, for example—work that has been influenced by Altschule's own findings—but he points out that they must be regarded as groundwork for further research, rather than as a contribution to clinical medicine. On the other hand, he feels that clinical studies of the effects of alcohol on real human beings are unduly focused on alcoholism and its psychology. The strongest federal interest in an alternative approach, he notes, has come from the military services, because of their reluctance to classify as alcoholic the many officers who need treatment for drinking problems.

Specialists in the study of criminal behavior have shown little interest in reaching out to physiology for answers to their questions. In the United States, criminology is a discipline founded upon sociology and psychology. Thus criminologists tend to concern themselves with the psychosocial roots of crime, and to ignore biological factors. In recent years the most important research in the latter field has been carried out in other countries, much of it in Scandinavia.

The most powerful force working against the application of biological science in forensic psychology, however, is fear—fear that science's thrust toward generalization will overwhelm the legal bulwarks guarding the liberty of individuals. There is reason to worry. In an earlier era, prevailing theories of inherited criminality led so steadfast a defender of civil liberties as Justice Oliver Wendell Holmes to uphold, in *Buck v. Bell,* involuntary sterilization of the mentally deficient. "Three generations of imbeciles," he declared, "are enough." More recently, as we have seen, advocates of psychosurgery could not resist suggesting eventual use of the technique to modify the behavior of noncriminals. The horrors of Nazi "eugenics" should be enough to persuade anyone of the potential danger to individual rights.

*

Courts that decide criminal insanity not only must evaluate evolving scientific theories while balancing individual rights but also must reconcile their judgments with prevailing policies of punishment. There are several basic justifications for penalizing criminals. One is the incapacitation argument, which holds that the primary purpose of imprisonment is to ensure that the criminal can no longer plague society. A second justification is deterrence, the idea that punishment will discourage the criminal himself, and other potential criminals, from committing further offenses. Rehabilitation theory, in turn, stresses the responsibility of the criminal-justice system to restore its charges to productive roles as law-abiding citizens. A less dignified but sometimes more powerful motive for imprisonment is simple revenge.

When judges impose sentences in conventional cases, they are not obliged to choose among these theories; criminal sanction may be warranted on a number of grounds. In cases of irrational violence, however, choosing and justifying an appropriate disposition can be difficult. Incapacitation may be mandatory for the defendant who still appears dangerous, yet may be unjust for one who is obviously cured. Moreover, as recent cases have illustrated, even if a court is convinced of a defendant's continuing madness, it cannot be certain that psychiatrists at the mental institution to which he is to be committed will concur in the diagnosis. When baseball star Lyman Bostock was shot in Gary, Indiana, in 1978, his killer was examined at a state hospital and found sane. He was then tried, acquitted on an insanity defense, and sent back to the same institution that had already attested to his sanity. Only intense pressure on the hospital staff prevented his immediate release.

Disposition after the verdict is invariably influenced by an earlier determination of sanity, for a court cannot be certain that a defendant will remain incarcerated unless he is held to be sane and sent to a conventional prison. If he is found not guilty by reason of insanity and committed to a mental institution, his fate will largely rest in the hands of psychiatrists, who themselves admit that they are not particularly good at predicting a patient's propensity for violence.

In 1980, Bradford Prendergast was committed to a Massachusetts hospital after having harassed a former girl friend.

Psychiatrists there, though acknowledging his deep hostility toward her, concluded that he was not dangerous to society at large, and released him, over the intense objection of the district attorney's office. Within days of his discharge, he burst into her family's home, kidnapped her at gunpoint, and dragged her to a secluded wooded area where he stabbed her to death. Such stories make front-page news. The release of inmates who go on to lead perfectly ordinary lives does not. It is not surprising that judges and juries are cautious about labeling defendants insane, and thereby entrusting them to the medical profession.

In the Decker case, Frank O'Boy argued for imprisonment, not on the basis of a need for incarceration (the record was unclear on this score) but on the grounds that the seriousness of the crime itself required stern punishment. A defendant found guilty of attempted murder must be jailed as a lesson to other potential offenders. Deterrence has always been a dominant principle in penal thinking, even though such subordination of individual interest to broad social aims contradicts other legal traditions. The eighteenth-century penological pioneer Cesare Beccaria recognized this contradiction. He concluded that punishment was an unavoidable evil, justifiable only if it was "public, immediate, and necessary"—and also mild, for certainty, not severity, was what deterred. (This sentiment is echoed in part today by those who advocate fixed sentences.) Philosophical doubts about deterrence apply with special force to insane offenders, for inasmuch as they cannot control their impulses, they are punished solely as examples to others. An important point about deterrence is that its effectiveness is a function of public opinion. Certainly one reason for the reluctance to accept insanity pleas in particular cases is the fear that this may be perceived by the general populace as "letting criminals get away with it."

As for the third justification for institutionalizing offenders, there is little opposition to the goal of rehabilitation, but widespread doubt about its success, whether it is attempted in conventional prisons or in institutions for the criminally insane. In both settings, efforts often have been perfunctory. Moreover, attempts to rehabilitate inmates through psychosurgery, behavior modification, and shock, drug, and fear therapies (the latter involving a drug that stops the prisoner's breathing) raise legitimate fears of institutional abuse.

The uncertainty of psychiatric diagnosis is thus felt not only in sanity determinations but in subsequent commitment decisions as well. That defendants are sometimes found insane suggests public sympathy for those afflicted with psychological problems, but convictions in famous cases, in the face of strong evidence of insanity, reveal the power of the contrasting point of view. The attraction of theories that root mental conditions in physical dysfunctions is obvious. To most people, "physical" equals "real." A defendant with a physical problem really does have something wrong with him for which he is not to blame, whereas one with psychological problems may be dismissed as having imposed them on himself. Moreover, physical problems are generally more susceptible to demonstration in court, although, as Charles Decker's case illustrates, this is not invariably true. Then, too, people have more faith in medical treatment than in psychotherapy. Even when there is no cure available (again, as in the Decker case), a judge or jury may be influenced by the seemingly better prospect that a cure for the physiological dysfunction will be discovered.

If one day medical science learns to identify physiological causes of violent acts, and if it devises cures for these conditions, then many of the current difficulties in disposing of violent offenders obviously will be solved. Rehabilitation will be possible and incapacitation will be unnecessary. Nothing we may expect in the foreseeable future, however, will fully free us from our dilemma. Cases like that of Charles Decker may begin to change our understanding of criminal insanity, but they do not bring about a revolution.

*

For years to come, insanity cases will be decided in a context of medical ambiguity. Although *Commonwealth v. Decker* likely signals increased reliance on physical evidence of mental abnormalities, psychiatry will continue to play an important role in many trials. What that role should be, of course, is very much open to debate. Psychiatrist Karl Menninger, one of the most influential members of his profession, praised Judge Bazelon's 1954 *Durham* decision for opening the legal process to scientific findings, but by 1968 he, like Bazelon's own court, had altered his position. "We psychiatrists should keep out of the court-room," he wrote in a book entitled *The Crime of Punishment.* "We don't belong there." Concerned about the integrity of psychiatry, he denounced criminal-irresponsibility trials as "a fraudulent, discriminatory, undemocratic procedure" in which mental-health experts were forced to twist their ideas to fit legal categories for the benefit of individual defendants. Other critics of the present status of the insanity defense have focused their attacks on what they see as undue weight given to psychiatric considerations by the courts.

Thomas Szasz, the best-known opponent of the existing system, has proposed the most drastic reform. Not only would he abolish insanity as a legal defense, he would altogether sweep away what he calls "the myth of mental illness." Only physical illnesses are real, the Hungarian-born psychiatrist insists, and no mental illness can be physical. The delusions of the "insane" person, self-created and useful to him, are merely lies. Szasz accuses his colleagues of propagating the myth in order to imprison and degrade those they disapprove of, and of lending their undeserved power to the state for the repression of individual rights. The scientific rationale for these claims is being constantly undermined by advances in biopsychiatry, however. Schizophrenia, for example, is Szasz's classic example of a "mythical" mental illness, but Professor Seymour Kety of Harvard Medical School, who directs research on the disease at McLean, gibes that schizophrenia seems to be "a myth with a significant genetic component." In any event, Szasz has pro-voked an important philosophical debate. What he advocates is a radical libertarianism—he would allow psychosurgery "be-tween consenting adults." The patients'-rights movement he has inspired is particularly necessary, given that much mental illness may, after all, be physiogenic and may thus be amenable to physical cures.

Short of abolishing the insanity defense outright, there are other measures that could bring significant change. One approach that is gaining support is to modify the legal process so that criminal guilt and criminal responsibility are regarded as distinct issues. In several jurisdictions there are now two separate proceedings when the question of insanity is raised. The first is a conventional trial to determine whether the defendant committed the offense; the second is a hearing to discover whether the defendant, if found guilty, lacked the mental capacity to be held responsible. (In the Decker case, Roseman's strategy of all but conceding the crime and emphasizing the irresponsibility defense can be seen as the lawyer's attempt to fabricate this two-step process, even though it is not contemplated by Massachusetts law.)

A somewhat different approach has been used in New Hampshire, where a panel of experts decides the issue of mental capacity in advance of the conventional trial. In still other states, there is a movement to change not the procedure but the judgments it produces. The traditional verdict of "not guilty by reason of insanity" has been replaced with a verdict of "guilty but insane." This semantic change is intended to emphasize that the defendant did in fact commit an illegal act, and thus placate a general public that often has been hostile to special dispensation for those with mental infirmities. A special presidential commission on law enforcement, headed by former attorney general Griffin Bell, issued a report in August 1981 that endorsed adoption of this new verdict in federal courts.

In 1981, the California legislature enacted a law eliminating the "diminished capacity" defense. Among other things, the bill was a response to the light sentence Dan White received in his trial for the murder of Mayor George Moscone and Supervisor Harvey Milk of San Francisco. White had claimed that he was under an emotional strain that was exacerbated by a junk-food diet. In signing the bill, California Governor Edmund Brown, Jr., declared that it would "end some of the ridiculous outcomes we read about." Although the law was passed with just one opposing vote, there are some lawyers who question its constitutionality, particularly the legality of a provision that bars psychiatrists from stating conclusions about defendants they did not examine at the time of the crime. Court challenges are sure to come.

New legislation may or may not make the administration of justice more certain and evenhanded. No matter how well the new laws work, the legal system must still confront psychological issues. Sanity and insanity, responsibility and irresponsibility, are legal terms, not medical ones. The lines that must be drawn between these terms are legal boundaries. There is broad public opinion that courts draw the lines too leniently and that insanity defenses are often based on feigned madness or bought expert testimony. Yet the best-publicized insanity cases, those involving wealthy defendants, famous victims, or particularly atrocious crimes, often serve to remind us how strictly our courts define criminal irresponsibility.

At the same time that Charles Decker's future was hanging in the balance in a Massachusetts courtroom, a young woman was standing trial three thousand miles away. She too came from a respectable family, she too was accused of a very serious crime, and she too relied on a claim of criminal irresponsibility for her defense. Patty Hearst's lawyers, however, advanced the so-called Stockholm syndrome—a captive's eventual self-identification with her captors—to explain her participation in the crimes of the Symbionese Liberation Army. Although she had been locked in a closet for days, then subjected to unspeakable physical and emotional abuse, the jury was unsympathetic and convicted her. Perhaps as the daughter of a privileged family, she was held to a higher standard; the jury may have regarded the claim that she had been brainwashed as indication of a weakness in her character.

David Berkowitz, the "Son of Sam" killer who turned his .44 on couples in which the woman resembled his ex–girl friend, seemed insane even to the police officers who arrested him. He received the word of God from old Jimi Hendrix records and his neighbor's dog; he wrote obsessed poems and kept a diary in which he claimed responsibility for hundreds of fires, many of which investigators proved he could not have set. Both before and after his arrest, the press and the public routinely called him "crazy," but he was ruled fit to stand trial, and was convicted and sentenced to confinement in an ordinary prison. The monstrosity of his acts was both compelling evidence of his madness and overpowering grounds for his punishment.

More recently, Marine Private Robert Garwood, court-martialed for collaboration while a prisoner of war, argued that his captors had used torture to destroy his will to resist. The key to Garwood's defense was that his unfortunate childhood had rendered him unable to endure beatings and mistreatment. The military court agreed that torture could be tantamount to a traditional insanity defense, and admitted that no POW could always live up to the letter of the code of conduct for prisoners, yet it declared the need to draw a line, to set an example for soldiers in future wars. Garwood was found guilty.

Of course not all insanity pleas end in convictions; even controversial psychological theories sometimes win acquittal. In a Florida courtroom in 1981, Juanita Maxwell, a quiet nurse and loving wife and mother, altered her personality in the midst of her testimony and became "Wanda Weston," a hard-drinking, dope-smoking party girl who admitted that she had beaten to death a nursing-home patient. Initially, the judge was skeptical, but he ultimately concluded that the defendant was too unsophisticated to fake such a convincing display of multiple personality. He found her innocent, and ordered her institutionalized for treatment, as her lawyer had requested. In another case, an admitted murderer was acquitted and released when psychiatrists persuaded the court that the personality in which he had committed the crime no longer existed.

In 1981, a Colorado man convicted of sexually molesting a young boy won a new trial after undergoing brain surgery intended to control his behavior. The defendant had not claimed insanity originally, because two psychiatrists had found him sane, but a later neurological examination revealed a lesion in the right frontal temporal lobe of the brain, the area related to sexual impulses. This new discovery, his lawyer successfully contended, showed that the man lacked the capacity to conform his conduct to the law. By excising the lesion, the surgeons in effect created a case of temporary insanity.

Late in the same year, Sadie Smith, a twenty-nine-year-old British barmaid with a record of more than two dozen convictions for arson, assault, and homicide, successfully avoided imprisonment for threatening to kill a police officer, by pleading that premenstrual tension had made her act out of character. All of her crimes, it was claimed, coincided with premenstrual phases that made her "a raging animal each month" unless she was treated with the hormone drug progesterone. In another case, a woman who had been charged with the murder of her lover used the premenstrual tension syndrome (PMT) to establish diminished capacity, and was put on probation for manslaughter.

These two cases have generated considerable controversy in England. One eminent PMT researcher (who appeared as a defense witness in the second case) contends that the syndrome is "clearly a hormonal disease whose symptoms no doctor would mistake." Experts do agree that hormonal fluctuations cause some physical or mental problems for forty percent of all ovulating women; for ten to twelve percent, the condition is so severe it requires medical attention and may interfere with their activities. Yet there is sharp disagreement over whether PMT can cause aggressive behavior, and whether it should be regarded as a legitimate legal defense.

Conditioning theory has sometimes been used successfully as a defense. In 1980, for example, two young men were prosecuted for smuggling massive amounts of drugs into Boston's North Shore. In separate trials, each defendant claimed to be a victim of posttraumatic stress disorder, or "Vietnam syndrome." They claimed that, unable to readjust to civilian life, they needed to re-create the sensations of military action by undertaking hazardous missions. One testified that he "had rather an addiction to adrenalin, to living on the edge." The disorder had been recognized by the American Psychiatric Association and had previously been used to win acquittals in cases in California and Pennsylvania, but the Massachusetts trials apparently were the first in which the syndrome had been invoked as a defense for nonviolent, premeditated crimes.

Even though the two men were involved in the same offense,

had similar battle experience, and raised identical defenses, one was found guilty and the other was acquitted. Perhaps the inconsistent verdicts can be explained by the fact that they were represented by different lawyers and appeared before different judges and juries. One panel may have felt that the defense was legitimated by the expert testimony that sixty percent of Vietnam combat veterans suffer from the disease, while the other may have been appalled at the prospect of granting criminal license to almost half a million people. In any event, these two cases in juxtaposition dramatically demonstrate that when insanity defenses rest on psychiatric evidence, verdicts are invariably subjective.

Taken as a whole, this catalogue of recent cases emphasizes the fact that irrational crime is a common feature of contemporary life. As much as we may wish to regard mass murders as utterly freakish, the fact is that the Atlanta murderer and John Wayne Gacy are merely the latest links in a chain that includes Charles Manson, Juan Corona, Richard Speck, Charles Whitman, and the Boston Strangler. We cannot predict the time and place, but we must face the reality that such violence will occur again — a reality that underscores our need for confidence that legal and medical institutions can accommodate conflicting interests and justly assign criminal responsibility. The most celebrated insanity cases, however, are poor tests of the adequacy of the defense generally. There may be a double standard of sorts that makes it harder for famous defendants to avoid conviction. No matter how earnestly jurors try to be dispassionate in judging a David Berkowitz or a Patty Hearst, they must know that they will be held publicly accountable for the verdicts they render. Likewise, a prosecutor who might be willing to accept a plea of diminished responsibility for an anonymous crime may in a publicized case feel compelled by public opinion to press ahead with a full trial.

*

Charles Decker was tried and sentenced in obscurity. The local paper had reported his crime, but did not cover the trial two years later. Like more famous defendants, however, Charles's mental state was investigated at a time when medical and legal principles were very much in flux. Yet in spite of imperfections in the system, the major participants in the case were generally satisfied with the outcome. Most gratified were Nicholas Decker and Mark Altschule. They feel that although Charles was found guilty, the defense "won" the case. They got what they wanted: The young man was not sent to prison but rather was permitted to undergo medical testing and treatment of his condition.

The elder Decker seems to interpret the outcome as a victory for science and common sense over narrow legalism. The opposition had to "keep up appearances," he feels, but he is convinced that everyone who understood his position was on his side. "Throughout the case," he says, "the police and the law courts helped me. If David hadn't gotten the boy off, I'd have threatened him, because his only 'antagonists' were in favor of him." Though he professes respect for Roseman and satisfaction with his performance, Decker insists that the lawyer "didn't work anything out—he asked what we wanted to do, and arranged it." Of course, Decker's view is jaundiced by the costs of mounting a legal defense. "Get me started on the way the system works, and the way lawyers make their money," he warns, "and I'll give you a tirade."

Mark Altschule shares his friend's impression. "Everybody was pulling for a solution that I had suggested, except Jonathan Cole," he says. He agrees (and on this point, even Cole is an ally) that the legal profession has much to learn about the efficient use of time. It was Altschule, however, who worked with Roseman to put the defense case together, and he has a different sense of how it was shaped. "I didn't plan any defense," he recalls, "I just told him what I thought was going on, and he used it in his own way." And he adds, "A lot of what I told Roseman he never used, which didn't bother me in the least. He was running the show."

On several occasions, attorneys representing clients accused of assault or murder have approached Mark Altschule seeking his services as an expert witness. They are planning an insanity defense based on physiological factors, they tell him, and have heard of his testimony in the Decker case. But even when the circumstances suggest a condition similar to Charles's, the physician has declined to appear. His involvement in that case was prompted by personal friendship, and by the fact that Charles had been his patient before.

Frank O'Boy, on the other hand, has been involved in several insanity cases since *Decker,* both as a prosecutor and, more recently, as a private attorney for the defense. By contrast, although David Roseman still does a great deal of trial work, it is almost entirely civil, not criminal. Thomas Dwyer is the one who, as a Superior Court judge, has had the most significant involvement in insanity cases, most notably *Commonwealth v. Gould,* a case with instructive parallels to *Decker.*

Exactly four years after Charles Decker beat the two teen-age hitchhikers with a hammer, Dennis Gould stabbed his former girl friend to death. Gould had a long history of crazy behavior. He had deliberately fallen in front of a moving train in order to amputate his own right arm. He had been in and out of mental institutions for years, but had been released after receiving therapy and drug treatment. He nevertheless persisted in believing that he had a divine mission on earth. He claimed that he had killed his girl friend because she was Jewish and that all Jewish women are "impure."

Judge Dwyer presided at the trial, but the case was also heard by a jury. The defense presented extensive psychiatric evidence, and even the state's expert conceded that the defendant could be schizophrenic. At the close of testimony, the defense asked Dwyer to impose a not-guilty verdict, but the judge sent the decision to the jury, and it found Gould guilty of murder in the first degree.

Gould's lawyer appealed to the Massachusetts Supreme Judicial Court, which ordered a new trial. The appellate court commended Dwyer for his "scrupulous" concern for the "problems raised by the defendant's mental illness," and acknowledged that some of its own earlier opinions might be inconsistent, but concluded that the judge should have instructed the jury that Gould's illness could have had a bearing on his capacity for deliberate premeditation. In any event, the outcome of the trial itself seems to confirm David Roseman's wisdom in forgoing a jury and avoiding reliance on psychiatric testimony.

When Roseman and O'Boy look back at the Decker case, neither has serious misgivings about his general strategy or his trial tactics. The prosecutor says that although he does not think his cross-examination of Dr. Altschule was his most "artistic" piece of courtroom work, he was generally satisfied with the results. He regrets being somewhat sarcastic with this witness, both for reasons of simple courtesy and because it may have backfired. He also wonders whether he might have gotten the physician to reveal the defendant's prior violence, if he had probed further.

David Roseman claims that were he to try the case again, he would still rely solely on Altschule's testimony, though he acknowledges that the choice not to use psychiatric testimony as well was a delicate one. Charles had been seen by a Dr. Bloomer at McLean, who was ready to testify that mental disease left the defendant incapable of controlling himself. But Roseman observes that "We believed that we had found the cause of the alleged behavior, that we could explain it in physical and biological terms, and that those terms were objective. We thought that would be the most effective way to present the case." At best, the lawyer figured, the psychiatrist would merely confirm what Dr. Altschule had already established, and at worst he would distract the court's attention from the unique nature of the case. Roseman had read enough appellate decisions to know that even strong psychiatric evidence may be disregarded. As became apparent at the sentencing hearing, however, Judge Dwyer likely would have welcomed such testimony. By coincidence, the judge already knew of Bloomer as an expert in such cases. Throughout the hearing, Dwyer emphasized his interest in the psychological dimensions of Charles's problem. Had Bloomer appeared, it is possible that the judge would have reached his decision about probation sooner. Whether he would have found Charles not guilty by reason of insanity is far less certain.

The one tactical decision over which Roseman and O'Boy

disagree is the defense's choice to waive a jury and try the case before a judge alone. O'Boy believes it was a mistake. Roseman insists that he would do the same thing again, noting that there were several important considerations that dictated the decision. For one thing, he was concerned that a jury might be overwhelmed by the circumstances of the attack—young victims, a sledgehammer, fractured skulls. "That's a pretty scary thing," says Roseman. "Now, will a layman accept an opinion—no matter how well founded—that the perpetrator of such an offense did so as a result of being sick, or is that too hard to swallow?"

Moreover, even if a jury agreed that Charles had a mental defect, it might regard him as so dangerous that he had to be locked up. Roseman's concern on this score is borne out by a 1981 Texas case in which a drifter was convicted of a half-dozen cases of murder, necrophilia, and cannibalism. The man had been in and out of mental institutions, where psychiatrists, making what seems a cautious diagnosis, had found him to have an antisocial personality. In spite of actions that showed him to be patently insane, the man was found guilty and sent to prison for successive life sentences, a result obviously intended to avoid any risk that he might be released in the future.

The most important factor for Roseman in advising his client to waive his right to a jury trial was the technical nature of the planned defense. Given the complexity of Altschule's research, the lawyer had to decide whether to trust the case to "a trained mind or a representative segment of the community." It was much the same choice, he notes, that faces a lawyer in an antitrust or malpractice case. He opted for the trained mind. "If I had to spend a year and a half to learn chemistry—and I was paid to learn it—how in God's name am I going to be able to educate a jury in just two days?" he says.

There were other considerations as well. Roseman had to consider not just a trial, but possible appeal. In theory, when a judge acts as the fact finder, his determinations are entitled to just as much respect as those of a jury, but in practice appellate courts are somewhat more willing to reverse a judge's actions than to appear to interfere with the traditional discretion of the jury. This is perhaps all the more true in highly charged and potentially controversial insanity cases. Furthermore, Roseman knew that under the *Ricard* decision, he would have no right to challenge prospective jurors on their attitudes toward mental disease and the insanity defense. Although he waited until the case was called to make the final decision on waiving the jury, he felt that the choice was actually clear.

Frank O'Boy acknowledges the legitimacy of Roseman's analysis and respects his counterpart for making the decision, but is equally sure that having a jury would have helped, not hurt, the defense. "I don't second-guess David—or maybe I do by saying it—but I don't think any judge sitting on the Superior Court would have bought his argument. And I think a jury might have." O'Boy believes that with a jury, insanity cases are won or lost in the lawyers' closing arguments. The evidence is important, but only to the extent that it provides ammunition for the lawyers. The judge's instructions and the law they expound may have little impact on jurors—an impression confirmed by a study in which different mock juries, given varying instructions based on the M'Naghten rules, the irresistible-impulse test, and the ALI standard, all reached virtually identical verdicts. "With a jury," says O'Boy, "I think it would have been up to the defense counsel to convince them not necessarily that there was some validity to the tests, but that you have a respected doctor, he's an expert in his field, he's taken this gas chromatography test and this flying enzyme test, and this is what they showed. In other words, convince the jury that you have raised a reasonable doubt." All it takes, he notes, is to persuade one or two people who will be influential in the jury room.

In some jurisdictions a defendant cannot waive a jury trial without assent from the prosecution, but in Massachusetts this policy applies only in capital crimes. The jury, after all, not only fulfills the individual's right to be tried by his peers but also allows expression of public sentiment on important social and moral issues. Notwithstanding the current enthusiasm for having expert tribunals decide technical cases, there is a strong argument for always having juries decide insanity claims, because beyond the medical issues there are unavoidable social choices involving the imposition of responsibility and the exercise of compassion.

Roseman himself admits that as a matter of personal philosophy he feels more comfortable with having a jury use its common experience to decide whether or not to accept expert opinion, but he is glad that in this instance his client was able to have the case tried before a judge. Had Charles been unable to waive a jury, his trial undoubtedly would have been different. Roseman would have taken much more time to bring out Altschule's testimony. O'Boy, in turn, says that he would have made sure to call both victims to testify, and that he would have placed much greater emphasis on the brutality of the defendant's acts. "There's an old adage, that when you're prosecuting a murder case, take a paintbrush and spread a lot of blood around the courtroom." Perhaps Roseman did make the wise choice.

Although O'Boy and Roseman have no serious regrets about the way they tried the Decker case, neither lawyer seems fully satisfied with its outcome. Frank O'Boy sees Charles's recent problems as vindication of his view that the defendant got off too lightly. "My feeling, with all due respect for Tom Dwyer — and I have great respect for him — is that he should have banged the guy with a term in Concord." O'Boy is still troubled by the case. "I'm not looking forward to it, but I wouldn't be surprised to open the paper some morning and read that Decker has killed somebody."

From the other side of the fence, David Roseman sees his client's continuing difficulties as confirmation of Altschule's medical diagnosis. Roseman expresses greater enthusiasm for the result. "We may have lost the battle, but we won the war," he states. In light of the two charges of attempted murder, it is true that his client could have received a much stiffer sentence. It is also true that Roseman was successful in winning the court's support for the medical testing Nicholas Decker and Mark Altschule so fervently wanted to conduct. But the disposition left his client with the stigma of criminal guilt, and put him under a confining probation order. After Judge Dwyer had announced his judgment, but before he imposed the suspended sentence, Roseman claimed his right to appeal to a higher court, though he never pursued it.

At first blush it is easy to criticize the court's decision as contradictory. Under Massachusetts law it is the prosecutor's duty, at least in theory, to prove that the defendant is sane. If Roseman's evidence did not raise a reasonable doubt in this regard, it may seem inconsistent for Dwyer to acknowledge in passing judgment that there was "an intriguing medical problem," and to use that problem as partial justification for a lenient sentence. Yet closer examination shows the judge's action to be a sensible response to artificially rigid insanity rules. In Massachusetts, as in many other jurisdictions, the insanity defense is an all-or-nothing proposition. One is either found guilty or acquitted. There is no middle ground in the law. In reality, however, there are degrees of mental incapacity — and degrees of certainty about its existence. In essence, Dwyer, not fully persuaded of the medical case but giving it some credence, found a way to improvise a rule of diminished capacity.

Judge Dwyer's finding of guilt also left the court in a better position to monitor Charles Decker's treatment and behavior. Had he been acquitted on grounds of mental incapacity, he still could have been sent back to Bridgewater State Hospital for further observation, but since the staff there had already declared that he was not suffering from any significant mental disorder, the institution probably would not have held him for long. Although a district attorney may contest the pending release of any inmate who has been found not guilty by reason of insanity, Frank O'Boy had no specific evidence that Charles would be a serious danger to himself or the community.

It can be argued that Dwyer's need to improvise a judgment was compounded by the peculiarities of the adversary system. It is beyond question that he had to make his decision on the insanity defense with less than complete information about Charles Decker's condition and history. A judge gets to see only what the lawyers choose to introduce, and this can be further limited by rules of evidence that rest either on considerations of proof or on the need to protect other interests, such as the constitutional rights of the defendant. When Dwyer decided the case, he had heard no psychological testimony about the defendant, a result of David Roseman's decision not to have Dr. Bloomer testify. Even witnesses who take the stand and swear to tell the whole truth do so only in a narrow sense. Mark Altschule, for example, a man of the utmost integrity, answered honestly each question that was put to him, but he was not in the least obliged to speak to matters that were not raised. Altschule knew about Charles's previous acts of violence—acts that were relevant to whether the defendant should have foreseen the consequences of drinking—but that issue came up only in passing, and the information was never put before the judge.

In an adversary procedure, the emergence of truth depends in part on the willingness of one side to challenge the other's evidence. Roseman knew that Gail Sussman's account of the attacks might not be true in some details. Charles claimed that the girls had goaded him, and it was not implausible that they had denied doing so to avoid seeming blameful in any way for what happened. Yet it was not at all in the defense's interest to suggest that provocation, rather than insanity, could explain the crime, so the girl's story was never tested.

Cases like *Decker* show that the court system can never find truth in the same way a laboratory scientist does, because the fact finder cannot have full access to information. But the establishment of truth is only one of several important goals served by the trial process, and these goals are often in conflict. If Judge Dwyer's full understanding of the case was hobbled by his inability to consider the information in the hospital reports, the state's interest (as well as the individual's) in encouraging candid conversations between inmates and their physicians was vindicated. The same rule serves the even larger purpose of preventing observation periods from becoming a means of inquisition. Moreover, while rules of evidence and cross-examination may exclude useful information, they do serve as a check against misinformation. The judicial system's quest for truth also must give way to the need to reach a decision. Dr. Altschule may be able to pursue his medical investigations until all the answers are apparent, but a judge like Dwyer must make a determination based on the information at hand.

A more troubling lesson of the Decker case is that equality of access to the courts is an illusion. Nicholas Decker ultimately ran up more than $30,000 in legal and medical bills to diagnose and defend his son; eight years after the crime, he is still paying off these expenses. Had it not been for his connections in the medical community, and had Roseman charged for all the time he devoted to the case, the cost easily could have been twice as much.

In his concurring opinion in *Brawner,* Judge David Bazelon wrote that "while the generals are designing an inspiring new insignia for the standard, the battle is being lost in the trenches." It makes little difference, he warned, whether the *Durham* rule or the ALI standard is used, if a large class of people lack the means to prove their case under either test. The courts have not let slip "our well-guarded secret that the great majority of responsibility cases concern indigents, not affluent defendants with easy access to legal and psychiatric assistance."

For every Charles Decker, there are countless others whose violence has never been evaluated, whose health has not been considered, and whose fate has been ignored.

*Sources*
*Index*

# Sources

READERS who wish to learn more about the insanity defense and brain dysfunction must be prepared to investigate both legal and medical literature. We have not attempted a comprehensive bibliography here, but have selected references that suggest the variety of research on the subject. Most of these works are fully documented.

*Mind, Mood, and Medicine: A Guide to the New Biopsychiatry,* by Paul H. Wender and Donald F. Klein (Farrar, Straus & Giroux, 1981), deals only in passing with "explosive personality disorder," but is a valuable introduction to current knowledge about the physical causes of emotion and behavior. Morton Hunt's forthcoming *The Universe Within: A New Science Explores the Human Mind* (scheduled for publication in 1982 by Simon & Schuster) promises to serve the same end.

The key work for those interested in the surgical treatment of temporal-lobe epilepsy is *Violence and the Brain,* by Vernon H. Mark and Frank R. Ervin (Harper & Row, 1970); in the Decker trial, both the defense and the prosecution relied heavily on the ideas in this book. The legal and ethical ramifications of such treatment are debated in *Operating on the Mind: The Psychosurgery Conflict,* edited by Willard M. Gaylin, Joel S. Meister, and Robert C. Neville (Basic Books, 1975). William R. Russell's *Explaining the Brain* (Oxford University Press, 1975) is a very accessible introduction to the complex subject of brain structure and function. *The Brain: The Last Frontier,* by Richard M. Restak (Doubleday, 1979), is a report on the current revolution in brain research. In late 1981 the *New England Journal of Medicine* published a special report entitled "The Nature of Aggression During Epileptic Seizures" (vol. 305, p. 711). In the same volume (on p. 696), the journal also published Jonathan H. Pincus's "Violence and Epilepsy," a provocative critique of the other study.

Ysabel Rennie's *The Search for Criminal Man: A Conceptual History of the Dangerous Offender* (Lexington Books, D. C. Heath and Co., 1978) is an excellent overview of the intellectual history of criminology; part 5 of this book is devoted to current ideas about the physiological determinants of psychopathic behavior. *Psychoanalysis, Psychiatry and the Law,* by Jay Katz, Joseph Goldstein, and Alan M. Dershowitz (Free Press, 1967), focuses on traditional psychiatric theory, but remains an important examination of workings of law and medicine. Herbert Fingarette's *The Meaning of Criminal Irresponsibility* (University of California Press, 1975) is a well-organized introduction to the evolution of legal definitions of insanity, and their shortcomings. His more recent *Mental Disabilities and Criminal Irresponsibility,* coauthored with Ann Fingarette Hasse (University of California Press, 1979), offers a prescription for reform that has drawn mixed reviews; it does include a useful bibliography. Walter Bromberg's *The Uses of Psychiatry in the Law: A Clinical View of Forensic Psychiatry* (Quorum Books, 1979), has a chapter entitled "Convulsive States and Violent Crime," much of which describes the trial of Jack Ruby, who shot Lee Harvey Oswald. The use of conditioning theory, in this case the so-called Vietnam syndrome, as a basis for insanity claims is described in a note by Geraldine L. Brotherton, "Post-Traumatic Stress Disorder — Opening Pandora's Box?" in *New England Law Review,* vol. 17, p. 91 (1981).

Notwithstanding the advances of medicine and the changes in

legal doctrine, we found two histories particularly pertinent to contemporary problems. The first is Charles Rosenberg's *The Trial of the Assassin Guiteau: Psychiatry and the Law in the Gilded Age* (University of Chicago Press, 1968), which nicely illustrates continuing problems of scientific accountability and institutional competence. Sanford Fox's *Science and Justice: The Massachusetts Witchcraft Trials* (Johns Hopkins Press, 1968) may be read as a parable of sorts, reminding us of the consequences when deviant behavior is judged by rigid orthodoxy.

Looking ahead, it is virtually certain that the coming years will see a great increase in research in this area. Current legal writing can be located through the *Index of Legal Periodicals.* Its counterpart in medicine is *Index Medicus.* Though general in scope, a good starting point is *Law and Science, a Selected Bibliography,* by Morris L. Cohen, Naomi Ronen, and Jan Stephan (MIT Press, 1980).

# Index